Sempringham Studies

Britain 1916-1940

Andrew Thorpe

Sempringham *publishing,* Bedford

Cover. Landscape in transition: the London Brick Company works and Stewartby from near Ampthill (Sempringham Collection). Other illustrations: pages 8, 18, 19 35, 89 and 94, Illustrated London News; page 69 Mary Evans Picture Library; pages 33, 46 and 54 Punch Picture Library.

Sempringham Studies are distributed to booksellers by Central Books, 99 Wallis Road, London E9 5LN   Tel. 0181-986 4854.

Sempringham Books are available (post free) to schools, colleges and individuals direct (10% discount on orders of 10 or more of the same title): Sempringham Books, PO Box 248, Bedford MK40 2SP.

ISBN 0   9515764   7   X

First published 1998

Impression number   10 9 8 7 6 5 4 3 2 1
Year   2002   2001   2000   1999   1998

Designed and set by Sempringham publishing services, Bedford.
Line portraits by Stephen Odom.
Sempringham publishing, PO Box 248, Bedford MK40 2SP
Printed by Redwood Books, Trowbridge, Wiltshire.

Contents

Preface. Ways to use this book   iv

1   Overview and Issues   1

    Chronology 1914-45   4

2   The Legacy of the Long Nineteenth Century   8

3   Pen Sketches of Key Personalities   12

4   War and its Aftermath, 1916-22   17

5   Party Governments, 1922-31   27

6   National Governments, 1931-40   43

7   Social Change   58

8   The Economy   73

9   Foreign Policy, 1918-40   86

10   Historians and the Inter-war Period   98

11   Britain in 1940: Continuity and Change   103

    Further Reading   105

    Index   107

To student readers and their tutors

Ways to use this book

Our world was shaped by the history of Britain in the nineteenth and twentieth centuries. This book is an account of Britain's history in the twentieth century from the First World War, which accelerated developments which had begun and which created new problems, until the Second World War had started.

Textbooks are a resource of information and understanding. They can be read from beginning to end. This book is designed to enable readers to build up a picture of inter-war Britain. The first and last chapters give readers the perspectives which foster understanding and Chapter 2 presents the background to the period. Chapter 3 provides word sketches of the main personalities mentioned in the book. The core chapters, 4 to 9, are straight-forward accounts of political, social and economic history. For comments on how best to read these chapters read the paragraph below. The chronology, pages 4 to 7, is a reference summary of the main events.

Students' use of textbooks will depend on their study purposes. History books can be read from the first to the last page but, dependent on the study purpose, this may not be the best procedure. The core chapters, 4 to 9, are substantially self contained and *can* be read in isolation from the rest of the book. For these chapters read the 'Introduction' and 'Conclusion' first and scan the content of the chapters by referring to the subhead-ings. Then read and, as appropiate, note the chapter, or that part of the chapter, necessary for your study purpose. When you have finished reading you should be able to answer the 'Questions to Consider' at the end. Answers require your assessment and judgement which, supported or illustrated by selected information, will enable you to write good answers to course questions.

A History book is a contribution to debate about the past. Chapter 10 summarises the debate and is especially useful for questions which require an appreciation of historiography.

1 Overview and Issues

From World War to World War

As 1916 dawned, Britain was in its second year of war, allied with France and Russia against the Central Powers dominated by Germany. Twenty-four years later, in 1940, it was to be at war again, once again with Germany, although, by the end of that year, alone and without allies. The intervening period had been one of significant change, but also one which showed a degree of continuity with the period that had gone before.

The formation of the Lloyd George Coalition government in December 1916 demonstrated a new determination to win the war by whatever means necessary. Victory did come in November 1918, but at a great price in human terms, and also with an unprecedented level of state intervention in society and the economy. The country then faced a difficult transition to peace. The Lloyd George government remained in office until late 1922 and tried hard to ensure a smooth transition, but it was buffeted by political, social and economic pressures. The economy moved into severe recession in the second half of 1920, and unemployment rose above a million, never to fall below that figure before 1940. Unrest in Ireland led to partition in 1922, with the bulk of that island becoming almost independent and the six largely Protestant counties of the north remaining part of the United Kingdom. In foreign affairs, the peace settlements were difficult to obtain and enforce, and in one case (Turkey) the whole treaty had to be scrapped and a new one agreed.

During the 1920s there were signs that Britain was slowly beginning to recover from the aftermath of war. The readoption of fixed exchange rates embodied in the return to the gold standard in 1925 signified to many at the time that Britain was returning to pre-war 'normalcy'. However, some things appeared to have changed for good - in politics, for example, the decline of the Liberal party was confirmed, to a large extent, by its disappointing performance at the 1929 election, while Labour had formed its first government in 1924 and formed a second in 1929. Even so, the decline of the Liberals and the rise of Labour seemed to show that a two-party system, seen as essential for stability by many, was making a comeback.

The economy went into severe recession in late 1929, and by 1931 the Labour government was on the verge of collapse. Eventually, in 1931, a severe financial crisis led to a political crisis and the government fell, being replaced by a National government under the erstwhile Labour premier, Ramsay MacDonald. This new government went on to win a sweeping electoral victory and dominate British politics until 1940. Labour went into opposition, bruised by its experiences and having lost most of its ablest and best-known leaders. The National government presided over a difficult period. The economy finally began to pick up in early 1933, and was reaching a boom in some parts of Britain by 1936. But other areas, particularly those dependent on old industries like cotton, coal and heavy engineering, experienced a grim time. In such areas unemployment remained very high and social deprivation was widespread. It was only with rearmament against the renewed German threat, in fact, that the economies of such areas began to move out of depression.

During the 1920s there had been no very clear threat to Britain's position in the world. The United States, it was true, had emerged from the First World War much stronger than Britain, clearly taking over the latter's one-time role as the world's leading diplomatic and industrial power. But the Americans were largely isolationist, and posed no serious military threat. Other potential enemies were weak. However, the rise of Hitler in Germany, and the development of Japanese and Italian hostility, meant that by 1936 Britain faced the possibility of conflict with up to three major military powers at the same time. The National government carried forward a policy of Appeasement, trying to rectify the grievances of potential enemies and ensure that potential flashpoints were removed. However, this failed and in September 1939 Britain and France declared war on Germany following Hitler's invasion of Poland.

Through all this, Britain remained a country with a fair level of social cohesion and political calm. It did not always seem like this at the time. The first couple of years after the end of the First World War saw massive strike waves. The General Strike of 1926 seemed to some to be a threat to parliamentary democracy. The economic crises of the time were real enough, both to their victims and to the politicians who had to try to overcome them. Yet, for all that, there was no strong threat to the parliamentary system. Whereas continental Europe witnessed the growth of strong extremist movements, this was not the case in Britain. The Communist party never reached 20,000 members: the Fascists never exceeded 50,000. Britain entered the Second World War in 1939 with a remarkable level of unity and very little dissent, with a higher standard of living, overall, than ever before. Such facts cannot have been irrelevant to the determination of the British people to fight through against Germany to the bitter end, although it must be added that it is impossible to see how ultimate victory could have been won against Germany had not first the Soviet Union, and then the United States, become Britain's allies in 1941.

Issues

From the standpoint of 1916, a number of issues were significant, quite apart from the immediate question of whether or not the war could be won:

- How would the political confusion of the war years be resolved? Was there a place for party politics and, if so, would there be a reversion to a Conservative-Liberal model or would Labour be able to make significant advances? If not, would Lloyd George emerge as a kind of charismatic national leader?
- What would be the effects of the extension of the franchise to all men and some women in 1918?
- Would the parliamentary system survive?
- Even if it won the war, would Britain be able to 'win the peace'? Could a peace settlement be found that would satisfy the desire for revenge while also laying the basis for future stability?
- Would the State's role continue to expand, as it had been doing before the war and was doing to a still greater extent under wartime pressures, or would it be pushed back to a more limited, nineteenth-century role?
- Would the relative economic decline, noticed by many commentators since the late nineteenth century, continue, or would the world's first industrial economy be able to push itself to the forefront once more?
- Would the severe social strains of war and its expected aftermath create unbearable social tensions, or would a degree of stability be achieved?
- Would living standards improve for all, or just for a few?
- Would the British Empire be sustainable?

It is with answering these, and other, questions that the rest of this book is concerned.

Chronological Table

1914

Aug   Britain declares war on Germany and Austria-Hungary

Nov   Britain declares war on Turkey

1915

May   Formation of Asquith Coalition, including Conservatives and Labour

1916

Jan   Conscription introduced

Apr   Easter Rising in Dublin

July   Start of Battle of Somme; Lloyd George becomes War Secretary

Dec   Asquith resigns and goes into opposition; succeeded by Lloyd George as head of Coalition of some Liberals plus the Conservatives and Labour

1917

Mar   Tsar overthrown by revolution in Russia

Apr   United States enters war on side of Britain and France

Aug   Henderson resigns from War Cabinet

Nov   Bolshevik (Communist) revolution in Russia

1918

Jan   Lloyd George declares British war aims

Feb   Representation of People Act: vote given to all men over 21 and most women over 30

Mar   Bolshevik Russia makes peace with Germany; German offensive in west advances about 40 miles

June   New Labour party constitution commits party to socialism

Nov   Germany and Austria-Hungary surrender. Labour withdraws from Lloyd George's government

Dec   General election: massive majority for Lloyd George Coalition

1919

Jan   Opening of peace conference

Feb   Appointment of coal commission under Sankey

Dec   Lady Astor becomes first woman MP to take her seat

1920

Jan   Treaty of Versailles comes into force

Apr   Conscription abolished

Aug   Communist party of Great Britain formed

Dec   Abortive Government of Ireland Act passed

1921

Mar   Anglo-Soviet trade agreement

Apr   Start of mining lockout; railwaymen and transport workers refuse to support miners on 'Black Friday'

July   Miners return to work on owners' terms

| Dec | Irish treaty signed: partitions Ireland into 26-county Free State and six-county Northern Ireland which remains part of United Kingdom |

1922

Feb	Geddes report recommends large public spending cuts
Sept	Chanak crisis
Oct	Carlton Club meeting: Conservative MPs vote to abandon Coalition and fight next election as independent party; Lloyd George resigns, succeeded as Prime Minister by Law
Nov	General election: large Conservative majority; Labour emerges with 142 seats and MacDonald returns as leader
Dec	Irish Free State comes into existence

1923

Jan	Agreement reached with United States over repayment of war loan
May	Law resigns as Prime Minister; succeeded by Baldwin
Oct	Baldwin at Plymouth calls for protective tariffs
Dec	General election produces no overall majority for any party: Baldwin remains Prime Minister for the time being

1924

Jan	Conservative government defeated in Parliament; MacDonald forms first Labour government
Feb	Britain recognises Soviet Russia
Aug	Dawes plan on reparations agreed
Sept	Campbell Case blows up
Oct	Government loses vote of confidence on Campbell Case, so MacDonald calls an election, which results in a Conservative landslide

1925

Apr	Britain returns to gold standard
July	Government announces (on 'Red Friday') nine-month subsidy to coal industry to offset need for wage cuts, and sets up Samuel commission to look into the industry's problems
Dec	Locarno treaties agreed

1926

Mar	Samuel report published, recommending long-term reforms but also short-term wage cuts in coal industry
May	Miners are locked out, which leads to TUC declaring a General Strike; Strike ends in surrender after nine days
Oct	Lloyd George succeeds Asquith as Liberal party leader
Dec	Miners return to work on employers' terms

1927

| May | Trade Disputes and Trade Unions Act weakens legal position of trade unions |

1928

| Apr | Vote given to all women over 21 |
| May | Parliament rejects the Revised Prayer Book |

1929

May	General election results in coming to power of second minority Labour government under MacDonald
Aug	Young Plan on reparations agreed
Oct	'Wall Street Crash' in United States; restoration of diplomatic relations with Soviet Union

1930

Apr	Signature of London Naval Treaty
May	Mosley resigns from government over its failure to adopt his radical scheme to combat unemployment

1931

Feb	May Committee on public expenditure set up
Mar	Mosley forms the New party
July	European financial crisis coincides with publication of May report, predicting a large budget deficit
Aug	Collapse of Labour government over issue of spending cuts needed to keep sterling on gold standard; National government formed under MacDonald; Henderson takes over as Labour leader
Sept	Government cuts spending and raises taxes; pound forced off gold anyway
Oct	Liberal party splits into official Liberals ('Samuelites') and 'Simonite' Liberal Nationals. General election sees overwhelming victory for National government
Nov	Emergency tariffs imposed

1932

Feb	Opening of world disarmament conference
Mar	Import Duties Act passed, imposing a permanent system of tariffs on imports
Aug	Ottawa imperial conference agrees measures of imperial preference in trade
Sept	As a result of Ottawa, Snowden and Samuelites resign from cabinet
Oct	British Union of Fascists formed. Henderson succeeded by Lansbury as Labour party leader.

1933

Jan	Hitler becomes German Chancellor
June	World economic conference in London
Nov	Samuelites cross to opposition benches in Commons

1934

Nov	Special Areas Act passed

1935

Jan	Unemployment assistance board crisis
Apr	'Stresa Front' formed between Britain, France and Italy
June	Baldwin succeeds MacDonald as Prime Minister
Aug	Government of India Act becomes law
Sept	Abyssinia crisis: Hoare declares full British support for League of Nations

Oct	Italy attacks Abyssinia. Attlee replaces Lansbury as Labour leader
Nov	National Government wins large majority at general election
Dec	Hoare-Laval Pact leads to resignation of Hoare as Foreign Secretary. Election among Labour MPs confirms Attlee as party's leader

1936
Jan	Death of King George V; succeeded by Edward VIII
Mar	Germany remilitarises Rhineland
July	Outbreak of Spanish Civil War
Dec	Abdication of Edward VIII; succeeded by George VI. Public Order Act bans wearing of political uniforms like the Fascists' black shirts

1937
May	Chamberlain succeeds Baldwin as Prime Minister

1938
Feb	Eden resigns as Foreign Secretary; succeeded by Lord Halifax
Mar	Germany annexes Austria
Sept	Three meetings with Hitler (the last of them at the Munich Conference) Chamberlain accepts German annexation of the German-speaking part of Czechoslovakia (Sudetenland)

1939
Mar	Germany invades Czech areas of Czechoslovakia; Britain announces guarantee to Poland against aggression
Apr	Hitler denounces Anglo-German Naval Agreement; Britain guarantees Greece and Romania against aggression
Apr-Aug	Abortive negotiations between Britain, France and Soviet Union for an anti-German alliance
Aug	German-Soviet Pact of non-aggression
Sept	Germany invades Poland; Britain and France declare war on Germany

1940
Apr	German invasion of Norway and Denmark
May	British evacuate Norway. Chamberlain forced to resign after government majority falls sharply in vote of confidence in House of Commons. Succeeded by Churchill, who forms all-party Coalition.
June	Fall of France
July-Sept	Battle of Britain

1941
June	German invasion of Soviet Union; Anglo-Soviet alliance formed
Dec	United States enters war against Germany

1944
June	D-Day landings in France

1945
May	Germany surrenders
July	General election produces overall Labour majority of 146; Attlee forms first majority Labour government

2 The Legacy of the Long Nineteenth Century

In order to understand what happened in Britain between 1916 and 1940 it is necessary to look briefly at Britain as it had emerged from the 'long nineteenth century', the period from the 1780s to 1914.

Crucial changes had taken place in Britain during that period. It was transformed from an agrarian and rural nation to a largely industrial and urban one. In 1780, cotton and iron together had accounted for only 3 per cent of national income. Yet the process of industrialisation, which had proceeded fitfully since the mid-eighteenth century, continued. By the mid-nineteenth century Britain was seen as 'the workshop of the world', its prosperity resting, to a large extent, on the 'staple' industries of the so-called Industrial Revolution: coal, textiles, iron and steel, and heavy engineering, particularly shipbuilding. This development continued during the remainder of the nineteenth century, and other industries, like footwear production, which had previously been operating in an old-fashioned way now came more and more to rely on the factory system. As economic

Britain, the workshop of the world. The Great Eastern *under construction, 1857*

organisation became more complex and living standards rose, the tertiary sector - retail, services like banking and insurance, and so on - also grew.

As the latter decades of the nineteenth century progressed, however, Britain came under increasing competition from other countries. The United States and Germany had both overtaken Britain industrially by the turn of the century. Other countries were also beginning to industrialise, although they remained, for the most part, a long way behind. By the end of the long nineteenth century Britain's industrial pre-eminence had gone, and there were fears for the future which, in the event, were to be largely borne out during the inter-war period.

Industrialisation was linked to massive population growth during the nineteenth century. In 1801, the population of Britain (excluding Ireland) was 10.5 million. Between then and 1851 it almost doubled, to 20.8 million; and between then and 1911 it almost doubled again, to 40.8 million. By the latter year, the norm was still for large families. Birth and death rates remained high in comparison with what would follow during the inter-war period and afterwards.

The populace was increasingly urban rather than rural. The 1851 Census was the first to show that more than half of the population lived in urban areas, a figure well ahead of any other country in the world, and the process continued down to the First World War and beyond. Individual cities and towns grew dramatically. Greater London's population rose from 1,117,000 in 1801 to 6,586,000 in 1901. Over the same period, the population of Birmingham rose from 71,000 to 522,000; that of Glasgow from 77,000 to 762,000; that of Manchester from 75,000 to 645,000; and that of Cardiff from a mere 2,000 to 164,000.

British society during the nineteenth century exhibited signs of both continuity and change. Social power remained, to a much greater extent than is often supposed, with the old elites. The landed upper class retained most of its land and much of its power, although the latter was lessened by the removal of the House of Lords' ability to veto legislation in 1911. True, the middle class was now much more significant, socially and politically, than it had been a century earlier, but the idea that Britain was dominated by its bourgeoisie is a difficult one to sustain. At the local level, landed magnates often remained the kingpins. If, in retrospect, the decline of landed society can be traced from the mid-nineteenth century, it was not always apparent at the time.

The working class, for its part, had made some gains in the social power game, but these can be exaggerated. In 1914, only about 60 per cent of adult males, and no women, had the parliamentary vote at any one time: the Reform Acts of 1867 and 1884, while enfranchising many working-class men, had not created anything like universal manhood suffrage (although it should be noted that many middle-class men were also excluded from the franchise). Politically, the working class's significance had clearly increased when compared with the situation earlier in the nineteenth century, but the increase was not all that great, and working-class politics was channelled fairly successfully into the established pattern of politics without too much disruption. W.E. Gladstone, the giant of Liberal politics in the three decades between the 1867 Reform Act and his retirement in 1894, was able to appeal to broad sections of the working class; and, in so far as he and his party were unable to do so, workers turned to the Conservatives, whose patriotism, jingoism and hostility towards Roman Catholicism made them very attractive to many people. Although socialism had made some impact in Britain since its 'revival' in the 1880s, its appeal remained strictly limited, and even the Labour party, formed in 1900 as the Labour Representation Committee, was able to make only limited progress in the years prior to 1914 despite its moderate, non-socialist approach.

Indeed, party politics was far from being revolutionised in the years prior to the First World War. The Liberals, after a period of division, had come back into power in 1906 with a huge majority, and were able to remain in office as a minority government after the two general elections of 1910, dependent on Irish and Labour support. There were many problems for this government before 1914, but, under leaders like the Prime Minister, H.H. Asquith and the Chancellor of the Exchequer, David Lloyd George, they remained a potent force, and it is hard to argue that they were on the verge of political extinction or that Labour was about to replace them. For their part, the Conservatives were enduring difficult times under their leaders, Arthur Balfour (1902-11) and Andrew Bonar Law (1911-21), but they retained widespread support.

Over the period since 1789, the constitution in Britain had changed by degrees, but never very dramatically. The franchise extensions of 1832, 1867 and 1884 had gradually brought more people 'within the pale of the constitution', as Gladstone liked to put it, but, as seen on the previous page, the results were hardly revolutionary. The monarchy remained at the apex of affairs, theoretically, although its powers had gradually been whittled away. Even so, King George V (1910-36) was to intervene politically much more than any of his successors have so far done. The balance between the Houses of Lords and Commons had shifted towards the latter over the period, a fact underlined by the Parliament Act of 1911 which removed the Lords' right to veto legislation passed by the Commons, but the upper house was to retain a two-year delaying power over Bills passed in the Commons until the late 1940s, and was to remain significant during the inter-war period.

The nature of the United Kingdom as a state had not changed all that much, either, at least since the 1801 Act of union with Ireland. Ireland and Scotland had some elements of an independent existence, but were, to a large extent, incorporated within the United Kingdom. For Wales, there was even less autonomy: by 1914 all cabinets included a Chief Secretary for

Ireland and a Secretary for Scotland, but there was to be no Secretary of State for Wales, or Welsh Office, before 1964. The Irish situation remained one of the trickiest problems facing British governments. Attempts to pass Home Rule legislation, which would have given Ireland a degree of autonomy within the United Kingdom, had come to nothing in the 1880s and 1890s. A third Home Rule Bill was introduced in 1912 by Asquith's government: Asquith was dependent on Irish votes to keep him in office and the removal of the Lords' veto made it conceivable that the measure could actually be passed. However, the upper house used its delaying powers and the measure was only placed on the Statute Book in September 1914, when its operation was suspended until after the war had ended. In fact, of course, the events of the war years were greatly to intensify the divisions within Ireland, and ensure that, ultimately, nothing short of partition between a largely Protestant north-east within the United Kingdom and a larger and largely Catholic Free State in the remainder of the island would suffice. That, however, still lay in the future as 1916 dawned.

Britain, by the end of the long nineteenth century, had amassed a large empire. In retrospect, its sheer scope was astonishing. It comprised the colonies of white settlement, such as Australia, Canada, Newfoundland, New Zealand and South Africa. Extensive lands were held in Africa. India was also controlled by Britain, in part directly, in other parts indirectly. The Empire brought economic benefits and international prestige, but it also brought problems. Its very scale meant that it tended to involve Britain in conflicts with other powers. Indeed, the ententes with France (1904) and Russia (1907), while symbolic of a new attitude of friendlier relations in the face of a perceived threat from Germany, were concerned mainly, in their actual terms, with reducing potential flashpoints between the countries in areas of British imperial involvement. The very scale of the Empire also meant that any major European war in which Britain participated would involve, willy-nilly, sections at least of the populations of a large number of parts of the world.

Britain, at the end of the long nineteenth century, then, was a country with massive prestige, wealth, and sense of its own worth, but also one with significant problems, both apparent and concealed. The events of the period between 1914 and 1940 were to solve some of these problems, and exacerbate others.

3 Key Personalities

Stanley Baldwin (1867-1947)

Conservative MP, 1908-37; Financial Secretary to Treasury, 1917-21; promoted to cabinet as President of Board of Trade, 1921-2; Chancellor of the Exchequer under Law, 1922-3; Conservative party leader, 1923-37; Prime Minister, 1923-4, 1924-9, and (in National government) 1935-7; Lord President of the Council (and effectively deputy Prime Minister under MacDonald) in National government, 1931-5. The son of a Worcestershire industrialist, Baldwin was an innocuous backbench Conservative MP before the First World War, but then rose steadily up the hierarchy. His promotion to the Chancellorship in 1922 was largely due to the refusal of leading Coalitionists to serve under Law. He then had a further stroke of fortune when the death of Law meant a new leader had to be found, as the only viable alternative, Lord Curzon, was generally felt to be unsuitable. Baldwin remained party leader for 14 years, and was three times premier, although there were times, particularly in early 1924 and in 1930-1, when he came under very fierce attack from sections of the party and the Conservative press. Baldwin cultivated an air of rusticity despite being an industrialist. He played a significant part in moving the party towards the political centreground and playing down the more partisan aspects of Conservatism. He was often accused of lethargy, but he was a fervent believer in capitalism and parliamentary democracy, and what are often seen as his finest moments came in 1926 (General Strike), 1931 (political crisis) and 1936 (Abdication Crisis) when either or both of these seemed to be under threat. When he retired, in 1937, it was in a blaze of glory. However, he was later attacked for not preparing Britain for war.

Neville Chamberlain (1869-1940)

Conservative MP, 1918-40; Director of National Service, 1916-17; Minister of Health, 1922-3, 1924-9, 1931; Chancellor of the Exchequer, 1923-4, 1931-7; Conservative party chairman, 1930-1; Conservative party leader, 1937-40; Prime Minister, 1937-40. Chamberlain was the son of the industrialist and Unionist politician, Joseph, and younger half-brother of Austen. He became a successful industrialist and later Lord Mayor of Birmingham. His failure as Director of National Service ended in lasting mutual hatred, with Lloyd George. First elected to Parliament at the age of 49, he advanced rapidly after the fall of the Coalition, helped by the Coalitionists' refusal to serve under Law. In the 1924-9 government he was an energetic Minister of Health, introducing significant reforms of pensions, the poor law and local government. By 1931 he was emerging as Baldwin's likely successor. His long period as Chancellor in the National government was marked by a degree of cautious innovation, and he emerged as the strong man of the administration. As Prime Minister, he was anxious to 'sort out' European problems, in order to avoid war and ensure Britain could continue on the road to prosperity. Thus, he pursued Appeasement. However, this did not avert war, and he fell in May 1940. Even so, he served in Churchill's war cabinet until approaching death forced him to resign later that year. Chamberlain was a very able administrator and a popular figure within the party. However, a streak of self-righteousness made him enemies, and ultimately proved disastrous for his historical reputation.

Winston Churchill (1874-1965)

Conservative MP, 1900-4; Liberal MP, 1904-16; Coalition Liberal MP, 1916-22; Conservative MP, 1924-64; various cabinet posts, 1908-15; Minister of Munitions, 1917-19, War Secretary, 1919-21, Colonial Secretary, 1921-2; Chancellor of the Exchequer, 1924-9; First Lord of the Admiralty, 1939-40; Conservative party leader, 1940-55; Prime Minister, 1940-5 and 1951-5. Son of a prominent Conservative politician, he entered Parliament in 1900, having served as an army officer. His support for free trade made him switch to the Liberals when the Conservatives moved towards protection. He was forced out of government in late 1915 after the failure of the campaign against Turkey, and returned to the Army for a time before coming back under Lloyd George. He soon emerged as one of the key figures in the Coalition. After the fall of that government, he eventually rejoined the Conservatives, serving as Chancellor (1924-9). By 1929, though, he was generally felt to have been unsuccessful in the post. In opposition, he became disenchanted with the party's shift towards protectionism and a liberal policy towards India, and resigned from the shadow cabinet in early 1931. Thus, when the National government was formed there was no place for him. By this time his record as someone who had twice changed party, who had retained a commitment to free trade long after it had gone out of fashion within Conservative ranks, and his reputation for intrigue (especially with Lloyd George) all made him a deeply distrusted figure within the party. He did little, for much of the 1930s, to improve his reputation, and seemed destined to remain on the backbenches, a maverick and a failure. His attempts to lead rebellions against the government's India policy made little lasting impact, and his support for Edward VIII during the Abdication Crisis of 1936 seemed merely to confirm a reputation for poor judgement. For a long time few were prepared to listen to him when he warned of the threat posed by Germany, but as war approached, he began to rise in stature. On the outbreak of war he was appointed First Lord of the Admiralty, and succeeded Chamberlain as Prime Minister in May 1940. He remained in the post until after the end of the war with Germany in 1945. For many years, Churchill was almost above criticism due to his record during the war but, following his death, reappraisals began to appear which stressed the essential failure of much of his career before 1940. He remains, however, the most written-about figure in twentieth-century British politics.

David Lloyd George (1863-1945)

Liberal MP, 1890-1945; President of the Board of Trade, 1905-8; Chancellor of the Exchequer, 1908-15; Minister of Munitions, 1915-16; War Secretary, 1916; Prime Minister, 1916-22; Liberal party leader 1926-31. Lloyd George was born in Manchester but raised in Welsh-speaking North Wales. After working as a solicitor he was elected MP for Caernarvon Boroughs in 1890 and remained its MP for 55 years. A fine debater and orator, he served in the cabinet from 1905, from 1908 as Chancellor under Asquith. He held the position until he was put in charge of Britain's apparently faltering munitions production in 1915. Increasingly, he was seen as the dynamic force needed to win the war, and in December 1916 became Prime Minister with the support of the Conservatives, Labour and about a third of the Liberal MPs. However Asquith, who moved into opposition, remained party leader. As Prime Minister in wartime he was seen as dynamic, exciting and, ultimately, successful, and his Coalition won a sweeping majority at the 1918 election. However, his peacetime government was soon borne down by problems, and in 1922 a revolt of Conservative MPs forced him to resign. In 1926, after a difficult period, he succeeded Asquith as Liberal party leader. He immediately began to spend vast sums of money - taken from the Lloyd George Political Fund, which was largely made up of the proceeds of the sale of honours between 1916 and 1922 - on revitalising the party's organisation and policy. These policies included a vast scheme of loan-financed public works to build roads and houses and so reduce unemployment. However, the 1929 election saw relatively few Liberal gains, and the difficulties of supporting a failing Labour government over the next two years were immense. In the summer of 1931 he became seriously ill, and so was unable to take part in the formation of the National government. He came out against the government when it decided to fight a general election, and resigned the party leadership. During the early 1930s he spent much of his time writing, but returned to active politics in 1935 with his 'New Deal', a revival of the 1929 Liberal policies. However, this campaign made little progress. He made little political impact after 1935 and died ten years later. Lloyd George was a colossal figure in the politics of the period. He aroused great enthusiasm in many, but also dislike, distrust and even hatred in others. Baldwin, for example, saw him as a fraud and a crook, and this view was shared by many Asquithian Liberals. His private life was also seen as somewhat scandalous.

Ramsay MacDonald (1866-1937)

Secretary, Labour Representation Committee, 1900-6, and of Labour party, 1906-12; Labour MP, 1906-18, 1922-31; chairman of parliamentary Labour party, 1911-14, and leader of party, 1922-31; National Labour MP, 1931-5, 1936-7; Labour Prime Minister, 1924 (also Foreign Secretary), 1929-31; National government Prime Minister, 1931-5; Lord President of the Council, 1935-7. Born illegitimate in the Scottish Highlands, MacDonald was a highly enigmatic figure. After becoming disillusioned with the Liberals in the 1890s, he joined the Independent Labour Party (ILP). As Labour's secretary he worked hard to build the party up. As chairman (in effect, leader) of the Parliamentary Labour Party (PLP) before the First World War he was a keen advocate of continued co-operation with the larger and more powerful Liberal party. He dissented from the decision to declare war on Germany in 1914 and resigned as PLP chairman. Already distraught because of the death of his wife in 1911, he suffered great anguish when attacked during and after the war for his 'unpatriotic' attitude. In 1922, however, he was finally re-elected to Parliament and immediately won the leadership of the party. In 1924 he became the first Labour Prime Minister, and returned to Downing Street in 1929. However, he was frequently tired through over-work, and seemed aloof from colleagues. His brand of moderate, reformist socialism had no immediate answers to the world depression which hit Britain so forcefully late in 1929. When his government collapsed in 1931 he agreed to form a National government, but most of his party opposed the move. He was soon expelled from the party and condemned as a 'traitor'. At the 1931 election MacDonald led a government whose expressed aim was to smash the Labour party. As National Prime Minister MacDonald was hailed as a hero at first, but gradually his mental and physical condition deteriorated. He became a sad shadow of his former self and an embarrassment to his colleagues and National MPs. He was finally ousted from the premiership in 1935, and died shortly after Chamberlain had dropped him from the cabinet in 1937. MacDonald was an able organiser and could be an inspirational speaker; he also wrote numerous books and articles about socialist theory. However, he was probably past his best when he came to the premiership for the second time, and his aloofness from colleagues, and tendency towards indecision, made for problems. Undoubtedly, the loneliness he felt after the death of his wife was a major cause of many of his problems. Had he died in 1930 he would have gone down as one of the great heroes of Labour history: as it is, his name has almost always been associated, however unfairly, with 'treachery' for his 'desertion' of the party in 1931.

4 War and its Aftermath, 1916-22

Introduction

Britain had been facing serious difficulties before the First World War. On the whole, these were intensified still further during the first two years of the conflict. Just because Britain was at war did not mean that all its other problems disappeared - far from it. The most obvious challenge which faced Lloyd George when he became Prime Minister in December 1916 was to win the war, but there was a wide range of other problems during the next six years. In retrospect it can be seen to have been one of the most difficult periods in British history.

The Coalition and the War

The Lloyd George Coalition faced a grim situation. Whatever realistic prospects there might once have been for a negotiated peace had now gone. The war must be won, and that meant defeating Germany, which did not seem to be immediately achievable for the time being. The French, in particular, had almost been knocked out at Verdun, while the failure of the Somme offensive to do more than tie up the Germans suggested that there could be no early knock-out blow on the Western Front. But the prospect of achieving victory elsewhere was now even slimmer, following the failure of Gallipoli and taking into account the increasing weakness of the Russians. Perhaps the hoped-for entry of the United States into the war might bring about a new, more favourable balance of forces? Yet when Woodrow Wilson was re-elected as President there in November 1916, it was with a mandate to keep his country out of the war. The challenge, in short, was massive.

At the same time, though, the new government did have some advantages. For one thing, the Asquith Coalition had cleared the way on a number of issues. It had finally introduced conscription (compulsory military service) in January 1916. It had more or less resolved problems of supply, while maintaining reasonable relations with the industrial labour movement. In addition, the new government, just by being new, had a short honeymoon period. Press and public criticism was, for a time, stilled.

Lloyd George's government was broadly based. It included about a third of the Liberal MPs. The remainder went into opposition under Asquith, but their opposition was largely ineffectual. The Conservatives supported the government. So, too, did the Labour party. All in all, the

Document 4a. Field Marshal Sir Douglas Haig, Order of the Day, 11 April 1918
There is no other course open to us but to fight it out! Every position must be held to the last man: there must be no retirement. With our backs to the wall, and believing in the justice of our cause, each one of us must fight on to the end. The safety of our homes and the freedom of mankind alike depend on the conduct of each one of us at this critical moment.

new government was more representative of Labour and the Conservatives than Asquith's had been, and this meant that Lloyd George had a greater stock of goodwill upon which to draw.

The year 1917, though, was not a good one for Britain. The Russian Revolution of March 1917 began a sequence of events which was to take Russia out of the war early in the following year. The resumption of German U-boat warfare brought the country within weeks of starvation. And the failure of the attempted offensive at Passchendaele that May merely underlined the obstacles in the way of achieving the knock-out blow. The Americans, it is true, did finally declare war on Germany in April 1917, but their mobilisation was slow and it was clear that any military assistance on the Western Front would take some time to materialise.

One result was that the government found itself faced with a restive population and had to do something to remain in control of the situation. Direct measures were taken to try to reduce discontent, such as the introduction of rationing of certain basic foodstuffs. Price and rent controls were introduced or tightened. Even so, there was an upsurge in strike

The British front in Flanders, 1917

The Coalition and the War   ●

activity and the revolutionary events in Russia began to inspire a not insignificant minority of the working class. For the first time, war-weariness became a significant problem for the government to face.

In early 1918 the Germans decided to attack along a broad front in the west. They were fearful that further delay would merely allow time for the Americans to concentrate their forces on the Western Front and so begin to overwhelm them, and they had the benefit of men released from the Eastern Front following the surrender of Bolshevik Russia at Brest-Litovsk. The offensive began on 21 March. Suddenly the Western Front stalemate, which had prevailed since late 1914, was smashed. German forces advanced rapidly, by up to 40 miles. The French government was advised to withdraw from Paris to Bordeaux, and plans were made to evacuate the British army from France and Belgium across the Channel. It seemed possible that Britain would lose the war.

But it did not. The Allies regrouped, now under a single supreme commander, the French Marshal Foch. The Germans failed to reach their strategic objectives; their gamble had failed. In retrospect, their offensive can be seen as a last-gasp effort: they had now exhausted themselves. The Allies began, from June onwards, to roll the enemy's armies back. German morale collapsed. By August the Allies were advancing rapidly, and the German High Command, weakened militarily and facing massive domestic discontent, realised that it was beaten. With surprising rapidity, the war came to an end with the Armistice on 11 November 1918. By then, all of Germany's allies - Austria-Hungary, Bulgaria and Turkey - had been

Armistice celebrations outside Buckingham Palace

● The Coalition and the War

defeated. It remained to be seen what kind of peace could be engineered from the wreckage.

The Lloyd George Coalition, 1918-22

There had not been a general election for almost eight years by the time peace came. The British government clearly needed a fresh mandate in readiness for the peace negotiations. And the Conservatives (and Lloyd George in the absence of Liberal reunion) were keen to cash in on victory to secure another term in office. Therefore Parliament was dissolved and a general election called. Labour had decided not to remain in the government, although a few wartime ministers left the party and stayed in office.

The general election was held on 14 December 1918. Government candidates fought on the victorious record of Lloyd George's wartime government, and there was promise of a vigorous programme of social reconstruction. Labour and Asquithian Liberal candidates were often attacked as having been hostile, or at least lukewarm, towards the war effort - significantly, Asquith, and a number of prominent Labour leaders like Ramsay MacDonald and Arthur Henderson, lost their seats. Overall, the results were fairly unsurprising (see Table 4.1). The Coalition came back with a huge majority. Coalition candidates took 473 seats; 50 further Conservatives were elected. Lloyd George's Liberals took 127 seats. The largest opposition party was Sinn Fein which, however, refused to take its seats and set up the unofficial Dail Eireann in Dublin instead. The largest opposition party at Westminster was Labour, but its performance had been rather disappointing. The party had adopted a new constitution earlier in 1918 as a sign of its new-found total independence from the fading Liberals, but despite getting 20.8 per cent of the votes cast it won only 57 seats. It also lost many of its abler leaders, including Ramsay MacDonald, Philip Snowden and Arthur Henderson. The independent Liberals won only 36 seats, and many of their leaders, including Asquith himself, were defeated.

Table 4.1 General Election, 14 December 1918

	Seats	% of vote
Coalition Conservative	332	32.5
Coalition Liberal	127	12.6
Other Coalition	14	2.0
(Coalition)	(473)	(47.1)
Conservative	50	6.1
Liberal	36	13.0
Labour	57	20.8
Sinn Fein	73	4.6
Irish Nationalist	7	2.2
Others	11	6.2

Thus, the new Parliament was very unbalanced. On the one side was a glittering array of talent, buoyed up by the prestige of having 'won the war': Lloyd George, who remained Prime Minister; Law, in effect, deputy Prime Minister; Austen Chamberlain, Chancellor of the Exchequer; Lord Birkenhead, Lord Chancellor; Winston Churchill, Secretary of State for War; and so on. Facing them were Labour, under the dour Scottish miner, Willie Adamson, and the Liberals under another rather dull Scot, Sir Donald Maclean. It soon became clear that the real opposition in Parliament would come from within the Coalition's ranks, particularly from discontented Conservatives, but they were, as yet, in no position to challenge the government's dominance seriously.

The government's first year in office was one of solid achievement. Peace treaties were made with all the former enemy powers, although that with Turkey was to prove unenforceable. The economic situation remained buoyant, as the high demand and full employment of the war years were followed by a massive restocking boom which, combined with the rapid elimination of women from much industrial employment, meant that full employment among men was maintained. The idea of building 'A Land Fit For Heroes' had been a major plank of the Coalition's appeal in 1918, and a number of steps were taken in the area of reconstruction. Already, in 1918, an Education Act had been passed, increasing the school-leaving age from 12 to 14, and making other innovations. The 1919 Housing Act obliged local authorities to survey housing needs in their areas and promised an Exchequer subsidy for council-house building. Rent controls were extended into peace time. The scope of national health insurance was also extended.

Part of the reason for this generosity towards the working class was the government's fear of the potential power of organised labour. The Labour party's formal adoption of socialism in its 1918 constitution, the memory of the recent revolutions in Russia, and the massive increase in trade union membership (up from 2.5 million in 1910 to 6.5 million in 1919) all played a part here. Strikes had been frequent in both pre-war and wartime Britain, and there was no marked change in 1919 in this respect. The miners' threat of industrial action was enough to persuade the government to appoint a Royal Commission under Sir John Sankey to investigate reform of the industry, which had been taken under public control during the war. In September 1919, the railwaymen struck and won significant improvements in pay and conditions. And, in many other industries, workers struck for, and won, shorter working hours. The pre-war 'Triple Alliance' of miners, railwaymen and transport workers, by which each promised to support the others in industrial disputes when called upon to do so, was revived.

But pressure began to grow on the government to change tack. Middle-class discontent began to emerge. In particular, inflation soared. Yet this would have to be brought under control, not just to appease erstwhile

Document 4b. Treaty between Great Britain and Irish representatives, 6 December 1921

1. Ireland shall have the same constitutional status in the Community of Nations known as the British Empire as the Dominion of Canada, the Commonwealth of Australia, the Dominion of New Zealand, and the Union of South Africa, with a parliament having powers to make laws for the peace order and good government of Ireland and an Executive responsible to that parliament, and shall be styled and known as the Irish Free State.

---

government supporters, but also to enable Britain to start to move back towards the gold standard (the pre-war fixed exchange rate for the pound which based the value of sterling on the gold holdings of the Bank of England) which was a stated aim of the government. Therefore in April 1920, Austen Chamberlain's budget attempted to cool down the economy by budgeting for a surplus. Interest rates were raised from 5 to 7 per cent between November 1919 and April 1920. When this was added to the natural end of the post-war boom and a downturn in world demand for British products, there could only be one result: recession.

The post-war boom collapsed rapidly in the light of all these developments. By the late summer of 1920 the economy was beginning to nose-dive, and by May 1921 male unemployment stood at almost 25 per cent. Never again, before 1940, did it fall below one million. In a state of some panic at the prospect of large numbers of ex-servicemen being forced

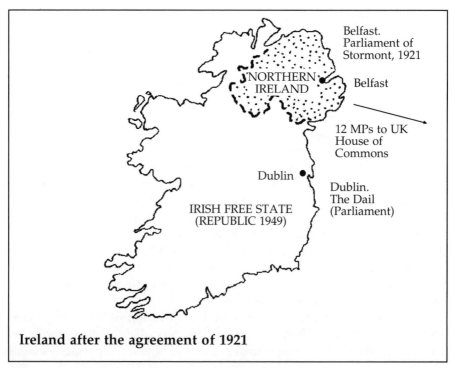

Ireland after the agreement of 1921

onto the Poor Law, the government extended unemployment insurance to virtually all industrial workers in 1920, and introduced 'uncovenanted' benefit, more commonly known as the 'dole', for those who had exhausted their right to benefit under the insurance scheme. These measures dampened down discontent, but little was done directly to try to solve the unemployment problem itself.

A major result of the slump was that the power of the unions fell sharply. Membership plummeted. While this weakened the industrial labour movement, however, it strengthened the commitment of many working-class people to political action through the Labour party.

The coal miners were a case in point. Before the war, and even to some extent at the 1918 election, they had not been especially pro-Labour. But the government's performance now drove miners towards Labour. The government, first of all, rejected the recommendation of a narrow majority of the Sankey Commission that the mines should be nationalised. Then, panicked by the economic downturn, the cabinet decided to bring forward the return of the mines to their owners to April 1921. The miners were determined to resist this, knowing that lower wages would result. They were locked out by the owners until they were prepared to accept wage cuts. Thus, they called on their partners in the Triple Alliance for sympathetic action.

But the Triple Alliance collapsed on 'Black Friday' (15 April 1921) when the railwaymen and transport workers refused to call a strike in sympathy with the miners. Their reasons were complex, but three main elements can be identified. First, Robert Williams of the National Transport Workers' Federation and J.H. Thomas of the National Union of Railway-men were anxious not to expose their members to the possibility of a long dispute, and subsequent victimisation, particularly at a time of economic difficulties when the employers were looking to cut their labour force in any case. Second, Thomas, in particular, was a moderate, and did not see the value of going into a strike which could probably not be won; he also believed that any such strike might be seen as revolutionary or, at least, a direct challenge to the government, and disliked the prospect. Finally, the miners' leaders themselves appeared divided as to whether they should oppose decontrol 'full stop' or whether some compromise might be reached. The result was that the miners were left to fight alone, and they were eventually defeated, being forced back to work on the employers' terms, after a three-month lockout.

Another result of the crash was the end of the social reforming impulse of the Lloyd George Coalition. As backbench discontent grew, and 'Anti-Waste' candidates began to make inroads into the Conservative and Coalition Liberal vote at by-elections, the government began to look for ways to cut back on expenditure, so that taxes could be reduced. The architect of the 1919 Housing Act, Christopher Addison, by now a hate

Document 4c. Speech by Stanley Baldwin at the Carlton Club, 19 October 1922
The Prime Minister was described this morning in *The Times*, in the words of a distinguished aristocrat, as a live wire. He was described to me, and to others, in more stately language, by the Lord Chancellor, as a dynamic force, and I accept those words. He is a dynamic force, and it is from that very fact that our troubles, in our opinion, arise. A dynamic force is a very terrible thing; it may crush you but it is not necessarily right. It is owing to that dynamic force, and that remarkable personality, that the Liberal Party, to which he formerly belonged, has been smashed to pieces; and it is my firm conviction that, in time, the same thing will happen to our party. I do not propose to elaborate, in an assembly like this, the dangers and perils of that happening. We have already seen, during our association with him in the last four years, a section of our party hopelessly alienated. I think that if the present association is continued, and if this meeting agrees that it should be continued, you will see some more breaking up, and I believe that the process must go on inevitably until the old Conservative Party is smashed to atoms and lost in ruins.

figure for most Conservatives, was demoted in April 1921 and forced to resign three months later. The ending of the 1919 housing subsidies and further spending cuts announced in the budget of April 1921, however, failed to satisfy the 'Anti-Waste' lobby. The result was that the government was forced to appoint a committee, under Sir Eric Geddes in August 1921, to survey the whole field of public spending and recommend cuts. Its report, in February 1922, recommended economies of 75 million, including cuts in education, the armed forces and other areas. While not all its recommendations were adopted, the budget of April 1922 did reduce public expenditure by about 15 per cent. With its two great social reforming measures - the Education and Housing Acts - now in tatters, the government's claim to be one of reconstruction and social reform looked very hollow indeed.

All this was bad enough. But there was more. Parts of Ireland descended into virtual anarchy between 1919 and 1921. Irish republican violence was met with brutal repression by the special forces (the 'Auxies', or auxiliaries, and 'Black and Tans') drafted in to restore order. The government's strong-arm tactics met with widespread condemnation on the centre and left of British politics. But some Conservatives were also antagonised by the ultimate solution, as embodied in the Anglo-Irish Treaty of December 1921, whereby Ireland was partitioned into a quasi-independent Irish Free State, comprising the 26 counties of the bulk of the island, and a separate Northern Ireland, comprising the six counties with substantial Protestant populations in the north-east, which had its own parliament but which would continue to send 12 MPs to Westminster.

A further cause of backbench discontent with the government was the image of what would now be called 'sleaze' that began to cling to it. This was exemplified by the growing outcry about the sale of honours, such as knighthoods and peerages. This was not, in itself, a new thing: both

Conservative and Liberal governments had given honours in reflection of contributions to party funds since the 1880s. But the scale and crudity of the process under Lloyd George excited outcry. When added to the rather tarnished image of leading ministers like Lloyd George himself, Birkenhead (an alcoholic) and Churchill, the honours' scandal aroused massive criticism. It did, however, ensure that the Lloyd George Political Fund became a major factor in Liberal party politics over the next decade.

The government also came to be seen as dangerously adventurist in its foreign policy. There was probably never a time when so many ardent imperialists sat around the British cabinet table. The result was that Britain had taken massive new territories, especially in the Middle East, as part of the peace settlement, to the extent that the British Empire reached its greatest ever territorial extent in 1921. But new territories brought new responsibilities and new dangers, and required high levels of expenditure at just the time when many people were calling for spending cuts. These concerns came to a head with the Chanak Crisis in the early autumn of 1922, when Lloyd George supported Greece's territorial claims to parts of mainland Turkey. Had it not been for the lack of support from the rest of the Empire, and the fact that the British commander at Chanak saw the futility of supporting Greek claims and made an agreement with the Turks, Britain might have ended up fighting a war against Turkey on behalf of Greek expansionism. Government backbenchers were appalled.

In the face of all these difficulties, the cabinet decided, in October 1922, that a general election should be called. Attempts at the 'fusion' of the Conservatives and Coalition Liberals into one party had floundered in 1920, so this meant convincing the two parties' MPs separately of the need to maintain the Coalition. This presented few difficulties for the Lloyd George Liberals, few of whom saw much future in reuniting with the Asquithians. However, it was to prove a different story where the Conservatives were concerned.

The Conservative leaders were not over-worried. Austen Chamberlain, who had taken over as party leader when Law had retired through ill-health in March 1921, believed that the party's MPs would be easy to convince, and was supported strongly in this view by Birkenhead. However, the meeting of MPs and peers, held at the Carlton Club on 19 October 1922, saw a different story unfold. Law appeared, and made a strong speech calling for the end of the Coalition, indicating that he would be willing to lead an independent Conservative party at the general election. Stanley Baldwin, a minor member of Lloyd George's cabinet, also made a memorable speech along the same lines. A vote was taken, and by 187 votes to 87 the Conservative MPs present voted to withdraw from the Coalition and fight the election independently of Lloyd George and his followers. The same day Lloyd George went to the Palace to tender his resignation to the King, and the post-war

Coalition - and, as it turned out, Lloyd George's career in government - were over.

Conclusion

When he left office, Lloyd George had been Prime Minister for less than six years. But they had been six of the most turbulent years in British history. The war had been won, but only after great sacrifice and struggle, and at enormous cost. The post-war Coalition had started brightly, but had ultimately collapsed amid recrimination and acrimony.

Politically, Coalitionism and its most ardent advocates had been rejected. The main focus for 'resistance' to 'socialism' and the more particular demands of the Labour movement would now be the Conservative party, standing alone. The force of Labour, though still seen as a potential threat, was now much diminished from its wartime and immediately post-war peak. The Liberal party's future was probably murkiest of all. The nine years that followed the fall of Lloyd George were to see a degree of confusion in British politics which were only to be resolved in the exceptional circumstances of the 1931 crisis and general election.

Questions to Consider
- Why did the Coalition win the 1918 election?
- Was 'reconstruction' anything more than an election slogan and a confidence trick?
- Could the Coalition have been viable in the long term?
- Can Lloyd George be blamed for the fall of the Coalition?
- So far as the Conservative party was concerned, what were the arguments for and against continuing the Coalition with Lloyd George?

26

5 Party Governments, 1922-31

Introduction

The fall of the Lloyd George Coalition provided a renewal of, rather than an end to, confusion between and within the parties. The period between 1922 and 1931 saw four separate governments come and go: two Conservative (1922-4 and 1924-9), which had parliamentary majorities, and two Labour (1924 and 1929-31), which did not. The confusion was increased by the dramatic swings in the fortunes of the Liberal party, and by the divisions within all three main parties. Ultimately, the period came to an end with the collapse of the second Labour government and the formation of a National government under MacDonald but comprising largely Conservatives and Liberals.

The Conservative Governments of 1922-4

After the fall of Lloyd George, Law formed a Conservative government. He faced two major problems. First, few of the former Coalition ministers would serve under him, Lord Curzon, who remained Foreign Secretary, being the only one of note. The brighter stars of the Coalition remained outside, and the new government had a rather undistinguished appearance. Baldwin became Chancellor of the Exchequer largely by default.

The second problem was the general election, which Law called as soon as he had formed his government. It was held on 15 November. The Conservatives were almost certain to win, given the weaknesses and/or divisions of their opponents; and Law, seeing that only the unpopularity of protection might stand in the way of victory, pledged that the government would not introduce general protection before a *further* election had been held. The Liberals remained divided; Labour, for its part, called for a significant extension of state control of industry, and a capital levy (wealth tax) to pay off the national debt. Nevertheless, Labour increased its representation dramatically, to 142 MPs, with a shade under 30 per cent of the votes. Many of the party's leaders, who had been defeated in 1918, now returned, most notably MacDonald and Snowden. MacDonald was elected leader of the party immediately after the election. The 115 Liberals were divided almost equally between Asquithians and Lloyd Georgeite National Liberals. The Conservatives managed to take only 38.5 per cent of the votes cast, but the divided opposition they faced meant that they emerged with 344 seats and an overall majority of about 70 (see Table 5.1).

Table 5.1 General Election, 15 November 1922

	Seats	% of vote
Conservative	344	38.5
National Liberal	53	9.9
Liberal	62	18.9
Labour	142	29.7
Others	14	3.0

After the election, Law moved away from Lloyd George's presidential style of leadership. Again in contrast with the Coalition, Law's government was largely content to wait on events. The main international crisis, the French occupation of the Ruhr in January 1923, was handled reasonably competently by Curzon and the Foreign Office. There was dissent from Law himself against the terms agreed by Baldwin with the Americans for the repayment of Britain's war debt, but the agreement stuck none the less. Otherwise, the government waited for better economic times to come. The one policy which might have been tried to improve matters, protection, had been ruled out by Law's pledge.

In May 1923 Law became seriously ill with cancer. It became clear that he would soon be dead. Many people believed that he would be succeeded by Curzon, the senior minister. However, Curzon was unpopular within the party, and his position in the House of Lords added to the doubts (Labour, the official Opposition, had hardly any members in the Lords). Eventually, therefore, Baldwin was appointed to replace Law.

At first, Baldwin continued with Law's policies and ministers. The one significant change, forced by his own elevation, was that Neville Chamberlain was moved from the Ministry of Health to become Chancellor of the Exchequer. Like Baldwin, Chamberlain was a protectionist; but Law's pledge at the 1922 election still ruled out a change in trade policy.

Any thoughts that the government would continue its 'wait and see' policy were soon ended, however. On 25 October, Baldwin made a speech stating that continuing high unemployment had convinced him that only tariffs could restore prosperity. This was a little misleading, since he had been a protectionist since the 1890s; and the speech did not, in itself, necessitate an election - it could, after all, have been passed off as a personal view rather than an immediate trigger to policy change. However, Conservative gut feelings had been unleashed. Baldwin had started a process which he probably could not have stopped even had he wanted to. In addition, he seems to have realised that protection would finally split the former Coalitionists from Lloyd George, who remained committed (in public at least) to free trade. It might be going too far, however, to argue that such a split was the original aim of Baldwin's speech.

With the protection genie released from the bottle, events pushed Baldwin towards a further general election. Polling took place on 6 December in what was, to a large extent, a free trade versus protection battle. The Liberals were uneasily reunited under Asquith in defence of free trade (but agreed on little else). Labour also focused on free trade, although also stressing the merits of socialism, nationalisation, and the capital levy. The Conservative share of the vote scarcely fell, Labour's share scarcely rose, and the Liberals polled 29.7 per cent, as opposed to a combined total of 27.8 per cent a year earlier. However, the position in the constituencies changed to such an extent that the Conservatives, while remaining the largest party in Parliament, lost almost 90 seats and their overall majority, emerging with 258 as against Labour's 191 and the Liberals' 158 (see Table 5.2).

Table 5.2 General Election, 6 December 1923

	Seats	% of vote
Conservative	258	38.0
Liberal	158	29.7
Labour	191	30.7
Others	8	1.6

All sorts of proposals came forward as to what should happen next. Some suggested a Liberal government under Asquith, who seems to have thought that this might have been a possibility because of Labour's weakness in the Lords. Others suggested a change of tory leadership to remove protectionism and the formation of a Conservative-Liberal anti-Labour coalition, although few tories were keen on a return to cross-party government. Some even talked of a 'businessmen's government'. In the end, however, events turned out fairly straightforwardly. The Conservatives met the new Parliament with protectionist proposals, which were inevitably defeated. Baldwin offered the King his resignation and advised him to send for MacDonald. MacDonald, who had led a moderate Labour campaign stressing the party's respectability and responsibility, accepted. The first Labour government came into office on 22 January 1924.

The First Labour Government, 1924

MacDonald's cabinet was mostly moderate in political outlook. The Prime Minister doubled as Foreign Secretary; Snowden became Chancellor; and Henderson took the Home Office. The various groupings within the party had representatives in the cabinet. There were seven trade unionists. The ILP left was represented by Fred Jowett and John Wheatley. The moderate Fabian Society was represented by Sidney Webb. There were a number of former Liberals, like Charles Trevelyan, and a former Conservative (Lord Parmoor). The party's weakness in the House of Lords helps explain why Lord Chelmsford was made First Lord of the Admiralty despite still being a member of the Conservative party. This was hardly the Bolshevik-style commissariat that strident anti-socialists had purported to fear.

But even if the government had wanted to push ahead with radical policies, it would have been unable to do so. Its position in the House of Commons was exceptionally weak. Not only did it not have an overall majority; it was not even the largest party. It would only take the Conservatives to vote against it, and the Liberals to abstain, to bring the government down. This fact led a few people to consider the idea of a Liberal-Labour Coalition, but there was reluctance on both sides. Asquith hoped that Labour would struggle and then give up, allowing him to form a Liberal government with Labour backing. Labour, for its part, wanted to squeeze the Liberals out of mainstream politics altogether, and so was hardly likely to offer the lifeline that a coalition would have represented.

At the same time, it suited no one to see the Labour government fall rapidly from office. The Liberals were prepared to support Labour because the alternative might be a protectionist Conservative administration, and because the Liberal party's weak finances and organisation made a further election an unpalatable prospect. The Conservatives, for their part, were in the process of reuniting in the face of a 'socialist' government, and the only danger to such reunification might be the stresses and strains of an early election campaign. Finally, MacDonald and his colleagues were also keen to avoid an early election. The left-wingers of the ILP argued that Labour should put up a radically socialist King's Speech, be defeated in the House, and then go to the country on a left-wing programme. But this would have cut across all that MacDonald and his colleagues had been trying to do: namely, to prove that Labour was 'fit to govern'.

This does not mean that the Labour leaders did not see themselves as socialists. It was just that their view of socialism was less excitable, and perhaps more 'realistic', than that of their left-wing critics. MacDonald, Snowden and their colleagues believed that socialism would come gradually, by a long series of reforms which would, almost without anyone realising, change Britain from capitalism to socialism. To achieve this, they believed, capitalism had to be prosperous - otherwise, how would the reforms be paid for? This meant that they should, above all, do nothing which would damage the mild economic recovery now underway.

This combination of parliamentary weakness and 'gradualism' meant that the government did not launch radical policies, such as nationalisation. There were minor shifts in economic policy: there was some increased spending, and Snowden refused to renew the wartime McKenna Duties (a policy which did some harm to the motor industry). Taxes were cut slightly, in the belief that this would release money for private investment and so improve the economic situation and reduce unemployment. In social policy, too, there was little radicalism. The most significant piece of legislation, Wheatley's Housing Act, provided subsidies to local authorities to build council housing for working-class people.

One aspect of the government's attempt to revive the economy was the removal of artificial barriers to trade. With this in mind, it was keen to negotiate a trade agreement with Soviet Russia. Talks began in the summer of 1924, but made little progress. However, the fact that Labour was talking to 'Bolsheviks' was a godsend to the party's opponents. Such controversy was soon increased by the conduct of the British Communist party, whose links to the Soviet state were hardly a secret, even if their real nature was scarcely understood. On 25 July, the acting editor of the Communist *Workers' Weekly*, J.R. Campbell, published an appeal to members of the armed forces not to fire on strikers. This was little more than the usual Communist rhetoric; soldiers were not racing around Britain at the time training their sights on members of the working class, on strike or not, and even if they had been, there was nothing to suggest that they would have taken any notice of Campbell. Regardless, the decision was made to prosecute him for incitement to mutiny. This aroused great anger in the Labour movement, and the prosecution was withdrawn. However, the Conservatives, now ready to fight an election, decided that this was their chance, and put down a motion of censure on the government. The Liberals, caught in the middle, decided to call instead for an inquiry. But MacDonald announced that if even the Liberal motion was passed, he would resign. Thus, when the Commons voted for an inquiry, an election was called for 29 October.

At the 1924 election, the Conservatives made much of the 'Red Scare', but otherwise their campaign was based around moderate, reforming Conservatism. Baldwin renewed Law's pledge of 1922 regarding tariffs. The whole party was now behind him, and the Coalition a rather distant, though certainly not forgotten, memory. Labour continued to stress moderation and respectability, and the party conference at the start of the campaign actually took further steps against Communist infiltration. The result of the election was curious. The Labour party actually increased the number of votes it received, and its poll share rose from 30.7 to 33.3 per cent. However, the 'Red Scare' atmosphere, the obscuring of the trade policy issue, and the continuing ineptitude and division of the Liberals, meant that the Conservative share of the vote rose dramatically to 46.8 per cent. The Liberals put forward many fewer candidates than in 1923 because of their financial weakness and Lloyd George's unwillingness to fund the party; their share of the poll almost halved to just 17.8 per cent. The Conservatives emerged with an overall majority of over 200 (see Table 5.3).

The first Labour government, then, had come to an end after just nine months. But it had been a significant interlude. It had shown, it seemed, that Labour could form a government. Its demise had marked the apparent end of three-party confusion and the return to two-party politics: few pundits gave the Liberals much of a future now. And, finally, Baldwin had used the short period in opposition to virtually complete the reunification of the Conservative party after the divisions and doubts of the Coalition period.

Table 5.3 General Election, 29 October 1924

	Seats	% of vote
Conservative	412	46.8
Liberal	40	17.8
Labour	151	33.3
Others	12	2.1

The Second Baldwin Government, 1924-9

Baldwin had managed to survive the disaster of 1923 with surprising ease. This was partly because he did not see any reason to resign, partly because of Conservative fears of renewed divisions at a time of a 'socialist' government in office, and partly because his demise might bring back the spectre of Coalitionism. Those who had supported him seemed justified by the sweeping victory of the party in 1924. In forming his cabinet, Baldwin was keen to bring back the Coalitionists, and to balance the government between right and left, protectionists and free traders. Accordingly, anti-Coalitionists like Curzon (Lord President) and Neville Chamberlain (Minister of Health) returned to important posts. But most of the former Coalitionists also came back. Austen Chamberlain was appointed Foreign Secretary; Lord Birkenhead became Secretary of State for India; and, in the most surprising move of all, Churchill, until recently a Liberal and still a free trader, was appointed Chancellor of the Exchequer.

Baldwin's main political aims were to preserve parliamentary democracy and capitalism. The best vehicle to achieve these ends was, he believed, a united Conservative party seeking to represent all anti-socialist opinion. He felt that, in the past, the Conservatives' problem, had too often been a tendency to alienate potential supporters by their partisan approach to issues like trade unionism, religion and trade policy. Accordingly, he set out to provide a new type of non-partisan approach - conservatism rather than Conservatism. If he emerged as the appeaser of the reasonable demands of the unions, a broad Christian rather than a narrow supporter of the Anglican Church in religious matters, pragmatic on trade rather than an ardent protectionist, and a pacifier abroad, then he would achieve this end, particularly if his government also passed 'useful' social reforms. In this aim he was also helped immeasurably by the departure of Ireland from the front rank of political issues following the creation of the Irish Free State in 1922.

In all these respects the first year or so of his second government proved a remarkable success. A back-bench attempt to introduce anti-union legislation was thwarted when Baldwin, in one of his most famous speeches, called for 'peace in our time'. In his speeches generally - a selection of which were published in 1926 in the book *On England* - he developed the themes of a broadly Christian, rather than narrowly Anglican, government, thus appealing to former Liberal voters, particularly Protestant Nonconformists such as the Methodists. The McKenna Duties were reintroduced in 1925, and a Safeguarding of Industry Act was also passed to prevent foreign dumping of excessively cheap goods on the British market; but a move to full-scale protection was ruled out by the renewal of Law's Pledge and the presence of the free trader, Churchill, at the Treasury. The Locarno Pact (see Chapter 9) seemed to mark an end to international tensions. And Neville Chamberlain got busy on passing the 25 pieces of social legislation that he had planned on entering office; in the end he carried 21 of them, among the most notable

Economic difficulties in the 1920s. A cartoon by Partridge in Punch *in 1925*
The Lady [a depressed British industry]. *Help!*
The Knight [Baldwin]. *Before I draw my trusty blade in your defence I must satisfy that your situation is sufficiently precarious to warrant my intervention. Be good enough therefore to furnish me with full and exact particulars of your necessity.*

● The Second Baldwin Government, 1924-9

being local government reform and a contributory pensions act for widows and orphans. With the economy gradually improving, the government signalled its commitment to a return to pre-war 'normalcy' by returning to the gold standard in April 1925.

But underneath all the apparent success of the first year of Baldwin's second government there was a time-bomb ticking away. This was the coal industry. Coal faced severe problems in the post-war period. To some extent these had been cushioned by low exchange rates, which made exports cheaper, and by disruption to foreign producers like Poland and Germany. However, the pacification of Europe and the return to gold changed matters. Facing the need to cut prices, the mine-owners announced wage cuts, and the intention to lock their workers out until they were accepted. The TUC responded by announcing a boycott on the transport of coal. On 31 July 1925, fearing massive economic and social disruption, the government announced a nine-month subsidy to maintain profits and offset the need for wage cuts. This was seen as a great victory for the unions, who christened the day 'Red Friday'. The lockout was cancelled, and a Royal Commission set up under the Liberal, Sir Herbert Samuel, to look for a permanent solution.

The Samuel Report was published in March 1926. It advocated a series of long-term changes to improve the industry's prospects, including the amalgamation of smaller mines. But, in the short term, it stated that wage cuts were essential. The miners refused to accept this 'jam tomorrow' approach, and also rebutted angrily the owners' demands for longer working hours. The result, as the end of the subsidy approached, was a stalemate. Small groups of ministers and trade union leaders met to try to reach a compromise, but none was possible. The owners posted notices that, after the end of the subsidy on 30 April, the miners would face lower wages and longer hours. The TUC, fearing a repeat of Black Friday, drew up plans for a General Strike in support of the miners. Last-minute negotiations failed to approach a realistic settlement, and the strike began.

In itself the General Strike was an impressive demonstration of solidarity with a million locked-out miners. On the first day, 4 May, around 1,750,000 workers in the 'first-line' industries - transport, printing, iron and steel, power stations, building and chemicals - struck. Engineers and shipbuilders were called out towards the end of the strike. But the strike did not have the desired effect. The government had been preparing for conflict, and managed to maintain supplies to all parts of the country. The TUC general council, faced with the point-blank refusal of the government to negotiate before the strike was called off, became more and more nervous about what they might have unleashed. Its aims were political, despite its disclaimers - it hoped to force the government to do something it did not wish to do, namely, to maintain existing wages and conditions. But they were not revolutionary. For a while, the TUC hoped that Samuel

Documents 5a. The *British Gazette*, 6 May 1926

The General Strike is in operation, expressing in no uncertain terms a direct challenge to ordered government. It would be futile to attempt to minimise the seriousness of such a challenge, constituting as it does an effort to force upon some 42,000,000 British citizens the will of less than 4,000,000 others engaged in the vital services of the country.

5b. The *British Worker*, 7 May 1926

The General Council does not challenge the Constitution. It is not seeking to substitute unconstitutional government. Nor is it desirous of undermining our Parliamentary institutions. The aim of the Council is to secure for the miners a decent standard of life. The Council is engaged in an Industrial Dispute. There is no Constitutional crisis.

---

might be able to broker a compromise settlement, but with the owners, miners and government all adamantly opposed to such a resolution, there was little that could be done. Faced with fears of a collapse of the strike and the widespread victimisation of their members, and the possibility of legal action against the unions, the TUC surrendered on 12 May. The miners remained out until the end of the year, when they were forced back to work on the owners' terms.

Solving the problems created by the General Strike

● The Second Baldwin Government, 1924-9

This was a victory for the government, but at a price. The economic results of the mining dispute were dire, with production and export earnings lost. Politically, too, the longer-term results were damaging for the Conservatives. Baldwin had tried to pose as a man of moderation, but the reaction of leading ministers, particularly Churchill (who had appeared almost bloodthirsty in his desire to beat the strike) went against this. So, too, did the passing of the 1927 Trade Disputes Act, which significantly damaged the legal rights of the unions, although not as far as some would have liked. Meanwhile, the strike's effects on the other parties were also significant. For Labour, industrial militancy, and the left generally, were discredited, allowing MacDonald and his colleagues to carry on their work of moving the party rightwards; while the disputes within the Liberal leadership that the strike brought resulted, ultimately, in Asquith's replacement as leader by the more dynamic Lloyd George.

More generally, too, the last two years of Baldwin's second government were disappointing. The spirit of Locarno lagged, and the breach of diplomatic relations with the USSR in 1927 seemed to signal a new era of international tension. Right-wingers like the Home Secretary, Sir William Joynson-Hicks, became more prominent. Pressure to introduce protection, or at least to radically extend safeguarding to major industries, grew. Meanwhile, the government ran into difficulties with its attempt to relieve industry and agriculture of much of the burden of rates (local taxation). 'Derating' was an attempt to ease the tax demands on the productive side of the economy, but it was easily misrepresented as a means whereby rich farmers and employers would be subsidised by ordinary taxpayers. Baldwin was aware of some, at least, of these problems. But he did little to ease the situation: in particular, he failed to reshuffle what was beginning to look like an old and somewhat jaded cabinet.

Meanwhile, both Labour and the Liberals were beginning to look like much more formidable opponents than they had been in 1924. The MacDonaldisation of the Labour party culminated in the adoption in 1928 of a new party programme, *Labour and the Nation*, which offered a very mild vision of 'socialism'. For their part, the Liberals, under Lloyd George, developed a radical set of policies to deal with unemployment in the 'Yellow Book', *Britain's Industrial Future* (1928). This put forward the idea of a programme of public works, financed by loans, to build roads and houses and so reduce the jobless total. Although open to criticism, the programme did offer a rallying cry to Liberals. In addition, the party organisation was pumped full of money from the Lloyd George Fund, and the party won a number of by-elections in 1927 and 1928.

With the 1924 Parliament nearing the end of its legal five-year term, Baldwin called an election for 30 May 1929. The Conservative slogan, 'Safety First', was intended to stress that the Conservatives could be

Document 5c. Labour party general election manifesto, 1929
We warn the electors against the misrepresentations of Socialism and the aims and policy of the Labour Party, which are already pouring from our opponents. The Labour Party is neither Bolshevik nor Communist. It is opposed to force, revolution and confiscation as means of establishing the New Social Order. It believes in ordered progress and democratic methods.

---

trusted, whereas both Labour and the Liberals were irresponsible and reckless. But this was rather unconvincing. In an attempt to revitalise his 'non-partisan' image, Baldwin renewed Law's pledge on protection, but this served only to antagonise many Conservatives. The result of the election was another hung parliament. The Conservatives took 260 seats with 38.1 per cent of the poll; the Labour party, with fewer votes, was favoured by the electoral system and emerged with 287 seats; while the Liberals, despite taking almost a quarter of the votes cast, emerged with only 59 seats (see Table 5.4). This was a poor result for the Liberals; although none of the party's leaders had expected seriously to win the election, they had hoped for more MPs. Even so, Lloyd George hoped to be in a position to bargain with both MacDonald and Baldwin, and to get electoral reform as the price of Liberal support. But it was not to be. Baldwin, who still took a very dim view of the Liberal leader, and who had no desire to help the Liberals survive, resigned immediately and told the King to send for MacDonald. The latter was appointed Prime Minister for the second time, on 5 June.

Table 5.4 *General Election, 30 May 1929*

	Seats	% of vote
Conservative	260	38.1
Liberal	59	23.6
Labour	287	37.1
Others	9	1.2

The Second Labour Government, 1929-31

The second Labour government began brightly enough. First, cabinet-making was fairly straightforward. Snowden returned to the Treasury, and Henderson became Foreign Secretary. Thomas was appointed Lord Privy Seal, heading a fairly high-powered team of four ministers to look at ways of reducing unemployment. Margaret Bondfield was appointed Minister of Labour and became the first female member of a British cabinet. Overall the new cabinet was even less radical than that of 1924. Second, there was little expectation of an economic downturn, even though unemployment remained above one million. And, third, a series of successes in foreign policy were crowned when MacDonald became the first British Prime Minister to address the United States Congress.

Indeed, foreign policy remained an area of relative success, with a naval treaty being agreed with the United States and Japan, and a date being set, largely thanks to Henderson's efforts, for the meeting of a World Disarmament Conference at Geneva. In some areas of domestic policy, too, valuable legislation was passed, with Greenwood's 1930 Housing Act introducing state subsidies for slum clearance and the building of replacement housing. Entitlement to benefits was liberalised.

However, such achievements were overshadowed by the economic situation. When Labour took office, unemployment stood at 1.1 million; when it left office, in August 1931, it was over 2.7 million. The underlying economic signals had been unfavourable from late 1928 onwards. Then the Wall Street Crash of October 1929 pushed things ahead with a vengeance. Unemployment rose every month in 1930. In the face of this crisis, which was common to almost the whole of the Western world, Labour had nothing to offer. Thomas's attempts to provide employment via limited public works and the encouragement of industrial reorganisation were pretty insignificant. The party leadership was baffled. MacDonald and Snowden had expected to build socialism from the success of capitalism, but had little notion of what to do when capitalism moved into crisis. All they could do concretely was try to apply the orthodoxies of old: attempting to restrain, and increasingly to cut, expenditure, to balance the budget, and to allow capitalism to restore itself to health.

There were those who dissented from this strategy. Sir Oswald Mosley, a member of Thomas's unemployment team, put forward a radical package of policies in the 1930 'Mosley Memorandum':

- A new small emergency executive, headed by the Prime Minister, would act like the old war cabinet in seeking and implementing solutions to unemployment.
- This committee would seek to implement a major transformation of British industry, shifting from reliance on export industries to emphasis on the 'new' industries producing largely for the domestic market. (By the time of the subsequent Mosley Manifesto, published in December 1930, this had hardened into a commitment to protective tariffs.)
- Loan-financed public works on roads, and so on, would mop up large numbers of the unemployed; in addition, more generous pensions and a raising of the school-leaving age would reduce the pool of potential workers. (See Keynes's ideas, pp. 82-4.)
- Interest rates would be cut in order to stimulate economic activity and make it easier for the government to take out the loans needed to finance public works.

Such policies had few supporters among ministers, economists or civil servants. They were rejected, in turn, by the cabinet, Labour MPs and the party conference. Their economic soundness was, and remains, debatable (see Chapter 8). In addition, even if the government had adopted Mosley's proposals, it is unlikely that they could have got enough Liberal support to pass through the House of Commons, since many Liberal MPs were now repudiating economic radicalism in fear at the scale of the slump. Mosley resigned from the government; the government decided simply to hang on and wait for better times. Ultimately, in February 1931, Mosley formed the New party. This was to prove the first stepping stone towards his formation of the British Union of Fascists, in 1932.

In the face of the slump, public, business and official opinion began to look increasingly favourably on protection as a way of at least slowing down the dramatic decline in Britain's industrial fortunes. Against this backdrop, the Conservative party's policy changed. At the 1929 election, Baldwin had renewed Law's pledge, but had promised some extension of safeguarding. After electoral defeat, powerful figures began to call for a rethink. These included back-bench MPs, plus leading members of the shadow cabinet like Neville Chamberlain and Leopold Amery, and the proprietor of the *Daily Express*, Lord Beaverbrook. By the summer of 1930 Baldwin's position looked shaky, but he saved himself by being persuaded, in the autumn of 1930, that the party should adopt a degree of protection. He was now, at last, convinced that a reversion to protectionism would not produce a repeat of the 1923 defeat. This, in turn, effectively put an end to MacDonald's tentative examination of tariffs, and the government remained committed to free trade.

For a while, the government's parliamentary position seemed reasonably secure. Baldwin's refusal to negotiate with Lloyd George had left the Liberals with little choice but to prop up the government, particularly since the Liberal party's finances were now in such a desperate state that an election was an extremely unwelcome prospect. In the aftermath of Mosley's resignation from the government, in May 1930, the Liberal leaders had begun to have regular meetings with ministers, and from October 1930 there seems to have been an informal arrangement in place, whereby the Liberals would keep Labour in office so long as it proceeded with legislation on electoral reform. Ministers seem to have hoped that they would be able to hang on for long enough for the economic situation to improve.

This said more about their powers of wishful thinking than about their political judgement, however. By the summer of 1931 the government was facing severe difficulties. It had alienated the left wing of the PLP, with about a dozen members of the ILP now acting as a separate group in Parliament. Mosley had already led a handful of MPs away into the New party. The trade unions were massively dissatisfied, angry that promised reforms had not been delivered. Core areas of support were also being lost. For example, large numbers of Roman Catholic voters were defecting because the government's education policies were seen as discriminating against Catholic schools. The party was in an organisational and financial

Document 5d. Cabinet minutes, 24 August 1931

Ramsay MacDonald tells his former colleagues of the formation of the National government. The new Cabinet would be a very small one of about twelve Ministers, and the Administration would not exist for a longer period than was necessary to dispose of the emergency, and when that purpose was achieved the political Parties would resume their respective positions. The Administration would not be a Coalition Government in the usual sense of the term, but a Government of co-operation for this one purpose. It had been agreed that at the General Election which would follow the end of the emergency period, there would be no 'coupons', pacts or other Party arrangements.

---

mess. Activists were demoralised. And, finally, the cabinet itself was ageing and acrimonious. Senior ministers scarcely communicated with each other: MacDonald's relations with both Snowden and Henderson were terrible by this stage. The parliamentary position was worsening, too: the Conservatives were working to force a split in the Liberal party, and having some success. Labour fared disastrously at by-elections after February 1930, and suffered massive reverses at the local government elections in November 1930. By the summer of 1931, therefore, the Labour government was faced with the prospect of collapse followed by heavy electoral defeat.

However, the way that defeat came about could not have been predicted. A European financial crisis and fears over the British budgetary position combined to suggest that Britain might be in serious financial trouble. There was a run on the pound, and Britain faced the prospect of being forced off the gold standard - something that terrified most opinion at the time. A series of cabinet meetings between 19 and 23 August could only agree tentatively to a 56 million package of spending cuts. This was not enough to satisfy the opposition leaders or international financial opinion that the budget would balance. But it was more than the TUC was prepared to accept: on 20 August the general council came out in opposition to all cuts (although they implied that they might be prepared to see cabinet ministers' salaries reduced!). Finally, on 23 August, the cabinet split 11 to 9 in favour of a 10 per cent cut in unemployment benefit. The minority, which included Henderson, was so large and powerful that the government could not go on. However, MacDonald was convinced of the need to remain in office and balance the budget, and on 24 August he, Snowden and Thomas joined a National government, supported by the Conservatives and Liberals, while Labour went into opposition.

For MacDonald and Snowden, the issue was clear. The only way to resolve the crisis was to make the cuts, balance the budget, and restore confidence. In addition, to make the cuts would be a supreme proof of Labour's fitness to govern: it would show that it was not beholden to any dogma, or to the TUC general council. This did not mean that he had to remain Prime Minister - he, and most others, seems to have assumed, almost to the death, that the Labour government would resign and be replaced by a Conservative-Liberal Coalition under Baldwin, which he would support from the back benches.

The bulk of the Labour party, however, saw things differently. Labour had always demanded full employment; failing that, the unemployed, seen as victims of an unjust economic system, were entitled to a decent level of benefits. To cut the benefits of the worst off in society offended this outlook. There was also a more calculating motive. Unemployment benefit underpinned wage levels: to provide an incentive to work, employers had to pay people more than they could get from the State for being out of work. For some time, employers had been trying to reduce wages in a wide range of industries. So it seemed to many Labourites that any benefit cut would be the signal for a general round of wage reductions. This all meant that all but about a dozen Labour MPs (who subsequently formed the National Labour party under MacDonald) went into opposition to the National government. Among party members, there was very little support for MacDonald's decision. However, Labour had been deeply compromised by its record in office and especially by the willingness of ministers to consider significant spending cuts (which would, for example, have reduced teachers' salaries by up to 20 per cent).

MacDonald's decision to remain as Prime Minister of a National government was not down to considerations of social climbing, a deep-laid plot, or any of the other motives which were suggested by aggrieved Labourites. The key consideration underlying his decision, as stated previously, was that the cuts needed to be made; it would, therefore, be dishonest to go into opposition. Further, King George V was keen to secure as broadly-based a government as possible to carry through what were likely to be highly controversial cuts, and in any case had come to like and respect MacDonald. Samuel, acting as Liberal leader since Lloyd George had fallen seriously ill, took a similar view, and also wanted MacDonald to stay to ensure that the Liberals did not become the prisoners of the Conservatives. Finally, the Conservatives themselves were reluctant, at this point, to appear to be cutting benefits without Labour support, since such an action could be portrayed as class legislation and so inflame social antagonisms. In addition, Chamberlain, and, more reluctantly, Baldwin, saw that MacDonald would be a good figurehead for a National government. For all these reasons, then, MacDonald told his shocked Labour cabinet colleagues on 24 August that, while the King had accepted their resignations, he would be staying on as head of a temporary National administration. This temporary government would last, through a variety of guises, for almost nine years.

Conclusion

The years between 1922 and 1931 had seen three main processes at work.

● Conclusion

41

The first was the attempt to restore party government following the Coalition years which had characterised much of wartime and the immediate post-war period. Both Baldwin and MacDonald had sought to edge the Liberals into obscurity, but the Liberal party had so far - despite appearances in 1924 - refused to go, and a three-party system remained in place. Linked to this, the second main feature was the battle for the political 'centre-ground': through their studious moderation Baldwin and MacDonald both aimed to gain this territory for their respective parties, while the Liberals tried to shore up their support. If this battle was still unresolved at the fall of the second Labour government, its resolution only had to wait for another few weeks until the sweeping victory of the National government at the 1931 election. And, thirdly, the attempt to return to pre-war 'normalcy' had resulted in the attempt to run down a wide range of state functions inherited from the war, the return to the gold standard in 1925, the maintenance (with modifications) of free trade, and the continuing attempt to solve Britain's economic problems by international agreement on issues such as tariffs, war debts and reparations. But this attempt had been of limited success even before 1929, and from 1929 onwards it had become increasingly clear that there would have to be something more than an attempt to return to 'the good old days' if Britain was ever to restore anything approaching economic prosperity. It was to be not the least of the National governments' achievements that they recognised this during the remainder of the 1930s.

Questions to Consider

- What factors accounted for the outcome of the general elections of this period?
- What were the main features of Baldwinian Conservatism?
- What were the advantages and disadvantages of Ramsay MacDonald's strategy of moderation and respectability?
- What, if any, was the significance of the Liberal party in this period?
- Why did the General Strike fail?
- Why was a National government formed in August 1931?

6 National Governments, 1931-40

Introduction

When the National government was formed on 24 August 1931, it was intended as temporary. Yet on 27 October it won the biggest electoral victory in modern British history, and remained in office throughout the 1930s. It only fell from power in May 1940, to be replaced by a Coalition government under Churchill. In some ways the experience of the National government was an unexpected turn in British politics; on the other hand, its uniting of the centrist instincts of both Baldwin and MacDonald, and the exclusion of the 'troublemakers' of the Coalition period, like Lloyd George and Churchill, can be seen as a logical result of 1920s politics (see Conclusion, Chapter 5).

The National Government from Formation to Election

When MacDonald returned to Downing Street from Buckingham Palace for the final meeting of the Labour cabinet, on 24 August, few of his colleagues expected to hear the news he brought - namely, that he had agreed to stay on as a head of a National government. He added that the government had been formed for only one purpose - to balance the budget in order to secure Britain's position on the gold standard - and that, when the necessary economies had been made, the government would dissolve and an election would be fought along party lines.

The new cabinet had only ten members, a sharp reduction from the normal size and a symbol of the 'emergency' situation. MacDonald was joined by three other Labourites, including Snowden and Thomas; four Conservatives, including Baldwin and Neville Chamberlain; and two Liberals, Samuel and Lord Reading (Lloyd George was recovering from a very serious operation, and was expected to be out of active political life for some time). The new government was supported by the Conservatives and Liberals, plus about a dozen Labour MPs.

The government introduced a new budget, which appeared to balance, and a National Economy Bill, proposing spending cuts of 70 million. This was a clever move because it involved only the 56 million of cuts that the Labour cabinet had provisionally accepted, plus the 10 per cent cut in unemployment benefits for which a narrow majority of the cabinet had voted. The markets were, for a time, reassured.

Documents 6a. J.H. Thomas (National Labour), election address for 1931 general election in Derby
I desire to make it clear that the changed circumstances are not brought about because I have changed my views, or because I have betrayed any trust, but because in the hour of the Nation's need I felt it necessary to stand by the country.

6b. Neville Chamberlain, speech at Birmingham, 9 October 1931
The late Government ... abandoned the ship which they had brought into such deadly peril. It was in these circumstances that the captain and mate and a few of the officers remained on deck in spite of the jeers and insults of the crew, and that Mr Baldwin fearlessly determined to go to their aid and join them in the effort to save the ship while there was yet time. He did not know whether greater credit was due to Mr Baldwin or to the Conservative Party itself, which shortly afterwards approved his action. He could not recollect any instance in our political history which would compare with the sacrifice of party interest made on that occasion.

6c. D.L. Davies (Labour), election address for 1931 general election in Pontypridd
The National Government has forced an Election upon the country to secure a majority for purposes it cannot define. Having failed in the objects for which it was formed, being acutely divided within itself, it seeks a mandate from you to continue its assault upon the poorer classes of the nation in the interest of a decaying capitalism.

The idea that the government might prove shortlived soon began to recede, however. Members of the government found they could work well together. The Conservatives, in particular, started to wonder whether a longer-term alliance might not prove successful. They began to see that most of their new-found allies were quite sympathetic towards protection. Snowden, the one convinced free trader among the National Labour cabinet ministers, had announced that he was retiring at the next election, while the Liberals were known to be on the verge of a split, with Sir John Simon and his supporters happily contemplating tariffs and the chance to take the places of the free trade 'Samuelite' official Liberals should the opportunity present itself.

In addition, Labour, in opposition, had swung quite sharply to the left, despite the efforts of its new leader, Henderson. Increasingly, too, the whole record of the second Labour government came under critical scrutiny, particularly as it began to emerge how far Labour ministers had gone towards making cuts in, for example, the wages and salaries of public servants (see p. 24). By late September, Labour's divisions and weaknesses were obvious. At the same time, it seemed increasingly that the best signal that could be given to calm the markets and restore financial and business confidence was for Labour to be hammered at the polls.

Therefore Conservative pressure for an election began. This was put to one side when Britain was finally forced to abandon the gold standard, on 21 September. The formation of the new government had steadied the markets a little, but only for a short time. Confidence in sterling remained shaky. Labour's strongly-voiced opposition to the new government caused the markets concern; there were fears that the government's position might not be entirely secure. A renewed banking crisis in Amsterdam added to a general air of anxiety. *The Times'* call on 16 September for an early election merely heightened foreigners' fears: might not Labour win such a poll? And, on the same day, all newspapers carried news that the Atlantic Fleet at Invergordon had refused to put to sea in protest against wage cuts. All this increased foreign withdrawals of gold dramatically. On Friday 18 September the Bank of England admitted defeat, and preparations were made to pass legislation, taking Britain off gold the following Monday (21st). In a sense, the departure from gold was a defeat for the new government. However, there was nothing that could have been done to prevent it; and the fact that it was a National government, pledged to balancing the budget, taking the step meant that confidence did not collapse. The pound fell from $4.86 to around $3.90, and stayed between there and $3.80 into November.

By November, a general election had taken place, and in its aftermath there could be no doubt as to the security of the National government's position. Soon after the departure from gold, Conservative pressure for an election resumed in a more intense form. Within a week, the cabinet was discussing the basis on which it could fight an election. The Conservatives hoped for a clear fight on the party's programme as formulated earlier in the year, that is, protection, imperial preference, and public economy. They knew that the Samuelites would not like this, but that was part of its appeal, for they wanted to get rid of the free traders. This did not happen, however. MacDonald wanted to retain the Samuelites as a counter-balance to the Conservatives, fearing that otherwise he would be seen as a tory stooge; while the Liberals, at the end of the day, had nowhere else to go. The result was that the Samuelites stayed and the government, much to the irritation of most Conservatives, fought on a 'Doctor's Mandate' programme, which allowed the government to consider all possible remedies to Britain's economic difficulties. Parliament was dissolved on 7 October. Polling was to take place on 27 October.

The 1931 election campaign has been the subject of much myth-making. Labour supporters often blamed stunts and scares for their defeat. But while MacDonald waved around German banknotes from the period of the inflation in the early 1920s, and the Liberal National (Simonite) Walter Runciman claimed that the Labour government had been putting the savings of small depositors at the Post Office Savings Bank at risk, such ludicrous claims were not the reason for Labour's defeat. In fact, Labour's leaders had been very pessimistic even before the campaign had begun, and things merely got worse. Labour's ex-ministers found it impossible to effectively counter the charge that they had run away at the time of the nation's crisis. They seemed dishonest because it was now widely known that, while in government, they had supported many of the cuts they were now opposing. Labour offered no ideas as to how new jobs might be created, and the party found that the great increase in unemployment under Labour in 1929-31 was a massive obstacle. Desperate for anything to say, Labour candidates began to talk about the need for 'socialism', but few of them had a clear idea of how it could be implemented. Defence of free trade was their other potential trump card: but with the growth in pro-tariff sentiment since 1929, this was not the vote catcher it had once been. Well before polling day, most Labourites should have been expecting a heavy defeat.

The government, by contrast, had a very positive appeal to many people. The 'National' tag suggested that it was 'above party', at a time

The support of the Conservatives to the 1931-5 National government, depicted by Bernard Partridge in Punch

when party governments were somewhat discredited after the problems of the period since 1922. MacDonald and his National Labour colleagues were praised as heroes. In addition, increased business confidence and cheaper exports following the departure from gold meant that unemployment was falling throughout the campaign. Not only that, but the Conservatives, with their protectionist policies, seemed to many voters to have the key to continuing the recovery. Protectionism was a vote-winner, in significant contrast with 1923. Labour's only remaining hope was that the government would somehow fall apart during the campaign, but this did not happen, although there were severe tensions in some parts of the country between the various 'National' parties. By polling day, the only question was just how big the government's majority would be.

The scale of the government's victory surprised almost everyone, though. With 67.2 per cent of the votes cast, it took 554 of the 615 seats in the Commons. Of these, 470 were Conservatives. Labour, with 29.3 per cent of the votes, took just 46 seats (see Table 6.1). Although the scale of Labour's defeat was exaggerated by the electoral system, it was a heavy defeat, none the less. For example, it lost all its seats in Sheffield, which had become, in 1926, the first big city to elect a Labour council. More than half its remaining MPs sat for mining areas: otherwise, it was confined to some of the poorest slum areas of London and a few other cities. The only former cabinet minister to save his seat was George Lansbury: he deputised as leader for Henderson, who had lost his seat, in the new Parliament. Labour's defeat was so heavy that it was almost inconceivable that it would be able to win the next election, and so the National government was ensconced in power for the foreseeable future.

Table 6.1 General Election, 27 October 1931

	Seats	% of vote
Conservative	470	55.0
Liberal	33	6.5
Liberal National	35	3.7
National Labour	13	1.5
National	3	0.5
(National government)	(554)	(67.2)
Independent Liberal	4	1.2
Labour	46	29.3
Independent Labour	6	1.5
Others	5	1.5

The National Government under MacDonald, 1931-5

With the election won, MacDonald formed a new cabinet of 20. It included, as well as the premier, three National Labour ministers; three official Liberals ('Samuelites'); two Liberal Nationals ('Simonites'); and 11 Conservatives. Baldwin remained in the honorific post of Lord President, essentially to act as deputy to MacDonald. Neville Chamberlain took over from Snowden as Chancellor of the Exchequer. Unsurprisingly, many Conservatives felt that they were under-represented, since they had over four-fifths of the MPs but only just over half the cabinet posts; however, this enabled Baldwin to keep out troublesome figures like Churchill and Amery.

The period up to September 1932 was dominated by the issues of protection and imperial preference. In December, emergency legislation was pushed through Parliament against foreign dumping, pending the conclusion of a cabinet committee's inquiry into remedies for the trade deficit. This committee, chaired by Chamberlain, produced its report quickly - as it had to, especially given that unemployment began to creep up again from January 1932 onwards. It was decided that the government would introduce a general system of protection. The level of tariff would be 10 per cent (later raised to 20 per cent) on most imports, although food and many raw materials would be on a 'free list' and imports already taxed (such as those subject to the McKenna Duties or the Safeguarding Act) would remain under those (higher) rates. In order to deal with the charge that tariffs would bring an air of corruption into public life, the day-to-day administration of the tariff was handed over to a 'non-political' body, the Import Duties Advisory Committee (IDAC). Then, in the summer, an imperial conference at Ottawa agreed to a limited system of imperial preference. It was hardly revolutionary. The Dominions, such as Canada and Australia, were developing their own industries, and did not want to be simply sources of raw materials and food for Britain and markets for British manufactures. Accordingly, it was agreed that an element of preference would be built into the Dominions' tariff arrangements by their further increasing their tariffs against all but British goods.

The political fall-out from all this was significant. The Liberal party remained committed to free trade. When the government agreed to introduce tariffs, the Liberals in the cabinet threatened to resign, but were prevented from doing so by an 'agreement to differ', which meant that, on this one issue only, Liberal ministers would be allowed to dissent publicly from government policy. However, this was an awkward fudge, and when the Ottawa Agreements made it clear that the system of protection was not entirely temporary, the remaining free traders in the cabinet resigned, to be replaced by a Conservative and a Liberal national.

This was all very embarrassing, not least to MacDonald, who felt that he was beginning to look like a prisoner of the Conservatives. Even so, the government's policies began, or so it seemed, to pay dividends. Unemployment peaked at 23 per cent in August 1932, when it has been estimated that around 3.75 million people were out of work. But it fell thereafter, with 1934 a particularly positive year in economic terms. While this was largely

Document 6d. Diary of Cuthbert Headlam, Conservative backbencher, 25 May 1933

The feeling in the Party is certainly a bit restless at the moment and, if Winston were not Winston, he would have a real chance of forming a big cave - many people who are not die-hards are genuinely anxious about the Indian policy and there are others who are tired of the National Government for various reasons - but I don't fancy that there is any real danger of a cleavage, or a revolt against Baldwinism, so long as Winston is the only alternative leader - as usual the fates are kind to Baldwin - what luck he always has!

---

due to a general world recovery, the government, by refusing to return to the gold standard and being able to maintain very low interest rates as a result, could claim some of the credit. Meanwhile, the cabinet pressed ahead with various reforms, as with the Unemployment Act of 1934 and the move to give a degree of provincial self-government to India. Conservative rebels disliked the 'National' tag, and there were rumblings against Baldwin, particularly over India, but there was little chance of a rebellion powerful enough to bring about a change in the party's leadership or its abandonment of MacDonald and the National government. This was not least because the Conservative seen as being most likely to lead such a coup, Churchill, was still widely distrusted within the party. It was for these reasons that the government's position recovered.

Meanwhile, the government's opponents could make little headway. Labour remained divided. While it was able to win some by-elections, and some by very large majorities, it was only regaining a few of its losses from 1931. The Samuelites, who, having resigned from the cabinet in 1932, finally moved to the opposition benches in November 1933, were even less convincing. Lloyd George, who had resigned from the party in disgust at Samuel's decision to remain in the government for the 1931 election, continued to be a brooding presence, but was now well past his best and spent much of the early 1930s writing his six-volume *War Memoirs*.

Anti-democratic forces made even less progress. The Communist party, which had been formed in 1920, remained relatively weak except in a few very localised areas, and its membership did not exceed 20,000 before the Second World War: at the 1931 election all 26 of its candidates were beaten, most of them very heavily (although it was to elect a single MP, William Gallacher, for a Scottish mining constituency in 1935).

The other extreme fared little better. Mosley's New party had been smashed at the 1931 election, and he went on to form the British Union of Fascists (BUF) in October 1932. For a while, the new movement prospered. With the support of Lord Rothermere's *Daily Mail*, BUF membership increased dramatically, to stand as high as 50,000 in the spring of 1934. However, the violent nature of fascism became increasingly clear. At the Olympia meeting that June, Fascist stewards brutally attacked hecklers; and, as the true nature of Nazism in Germany also became apparent,

Rothermere withdrew his support. Membership had collapsed to 5,000 by the end of 1934. Increasingly, Mosley allowed the BUF to become marginalised as a band of anti-Semitic thugs with little real support outside London's East End. A legal prohibition on the Blackshirt uniform in 1936 merely confirmed the movement's decline. The BUF was effectively finished well before 1940, when it was banned, and many of its members were imprisoned.

A significant part of the explanation for the failure of the political extremes was the performance of the National government. The government's economic strategy was not exciting. But it was fairly solid. At the Exchequer, Chamberlain maintained low interest rates, managed the exchange rate and tried to keep taxation and spending down. He also avoided radical moves to create employment through loan-financed public works. This was all in the belief that, ultimately, only private enterprise could restore prosperity. The main defeat Chamberlain suffered was when he was virtually forced, following a press campaign, to agree to a Special Areas Act in 1934 (see Chapter 8). The Act, though, was essentially a public relations exercise, and did not mark a radical departure from the government's basic economic strategy.

What underpinned that strategy, of course, was the unemployment benefits system. Compared with most other countries at the time, this was relatively generous. However, this became a controversial area in early 1935. The government's 1934 Unemployment Act had introduced various reforms, including the institution of uniform national rates of benefit for those who had exhausted their right to benefit under the unemployment insurance scheme. This new national system of 'assistance' was to be run by an Unemployment Assistance Board (UAB) which, following the example set by IDAC, was to take the issue 'out of politics'. Unfortunately, when the new scales of assistance were announced in January 1935, it was found that they were lower than those hitherto paid by many local authorities. The result was uproar, with civil disorder in some parts of Britain, particularly South Wales. Protest came, not just from the left and the unions, but from the Churches and even some Conservative MPs. The government was forced into a humiliating climbdown, being forced to overrule the UAB and pay whichever of the old or new rates of assistance was the higher.

This was something of a nine-day wonder, however. Chamberlain, whose idea the Act had been, emerged remarkably unscathed. The strength of his position was shown when, that spring, Lloyd George announced his 'New Deal', a revival of many of the 1929 Liberal pledges to produce jobs via loan-financed public works, albeit with a new title borrowed from the American President, F.D. Roosevelt. Although the cabinet went through the motions of interviewing Lloyd George about his ideas, and although there was speculation that the former premier might be asked to join the government, Chamberlain's veto of any co-operation with Lloyd George killed the idea. Meanwhile, other difficulties were being overcome. The Government of India Act, giving Indians greater say over provincial administration, was finally passed. This relieved the National government of an issue on which it had clashed repeatedly with a significant minority of its backbenchers. The economy continued to prosper, although with unemployment still over two million and some areas of Britain still very depressed. And Labour continued to be lacklustre in opposition. One remaining embarrassment for the government was MacDonald. He had been in decline for some time: his speeches had become more and more rambling, and he seems to have been suffering from some form of dementia. It was clear that he would not be fit enough to lead the government at the next general election, and so, following the Silver Jubilee in May 1935 to celebrate 25 years of King George V's reign, he and Baldwin switched offices. The Conservative leader became Prime Minister for the third time, on 7 June 1935.

The National Government under Baldwin, 1935-7

On assuming office, Baldwin carried out a limited reshuffle in readiness for the general election which could not be long away. Simon, widely perceived as a failure as Foreign Secretary, became Home Secretary and was replaced by Sir Samuel Hoare. There was, unsurprisingly, no place for Churchill. Overall, the 22-strong cabinet comprised 15 Conservatives, four Liberal Nationals, and three National Labourites.

The government's approach was, essentially, business as usual, in preparation for an election in the autumn. One potential area of trouble which emerged was Abyssinia. It became apparent, during the summer of 1935, that Mussolini's Italy was about to attack the independent East African state. However, in September 1935, Hoare made a masterful speech to the League of Nations Assembly at Geneva, committing Britain to supporting the League against Italy. It seemed that, at least so far as potential electoral embarrassment was concerned, the issue had been dealt with (see Chapter 9). With unemployment still falling, Baldwin called an election for 14 November.

There could be little doubt that the National government would win. In opposition, Labour had struggled to reassert itself, but had been divided and, at times, confused. Its 1934 conference had adopted a new party programme, *For Socialism and Peace*, but the 1935 conference, held on the eve of the election campaign, was far less productive and culminated in the resignation of the party leader. Lansbury, as a pacifist, objected to the party's support for economic sanctions against Italy. He was replaced - initially as a temporary measure - by his deputy, Clement Attlee. The Liberals were in an even worse state, so badly off for cash and personnel that they could only run 161 candidates. In what, it was generally agreed, was a quiet campaign, the opposition was on a hiding to nothing.

And so it proved. The National government, fighting essentially on a programme of 'Safety First' (although, with a view to the Conservatives' defeat in 1929, the slogan was not used) secured 53.3 per cent of the votes cast and took 429 seats (including 387 Conservatives). Labour fought on socialist policies of extensive nationalisation and socialist planning, as outlined in the 1934 programme. It recovered its poll share quite impressively, to take 38 per cent of the votes cast (actually higher than in 1929, when it had won), but the absence of three-way fights in the constituencies meant that this translated into far fewer seats (154) than it had done six years earlier (see Table 6.2). Despite the return of apparently 'brighter' figures, like Herbert Morrison, Attlee held on to the leadership in the elections which followed, and was, in fact, to remain in the position until 1955. The Liberals, who had little coherent to say that was not said better by the government or Labour, emerged with only 21 MPs and polled very thinly; their leader, Samuel, lost his seat. His successor, Sir Archibald Sinclair, was younger and more dynamic, but it was to make little difference to the party's dwindling fortunes for the remainder of the decade.

Table 6.2 General Election, 14 November 1935

	Seats	% of vote
Conservative	387	47.8
Liberal National	33	3.7
National Labour	8	1.5
National	1	0.3
(National government)	(429)	(53.3)
Liberal	21	6.7
Labour	154	38.0
Independent Labour	4	0.6
Others	7	1.4

In some ways the 1935 election was the highpoint of Baldwinism. In 1929, 'Safety First' had been defeated; six years later, an appeal on essentially the same lines was hugely successful. Yet almost immediately things began to go wrong. In the face of continuing Italian threats to Abyssinia, Hoare went to Paris and agreed, with the approval of the cabinet, a pact with the French premier, Pierre Laval, to partition the African state on lines supposedly attractive to Mussolini. The news leaked; there was a massive public outcry against rewarding Italian aggression; the cabinet repudiated Hoare; and the Foreign Secretary was forced to resign. Anthony Eden succeeded him. 'No more coals to Newcastle, no more Hoares to Paris' was the King's characteristically blunt summary of the unhappy interlude.

This joke was just about George V's last for, in January 1936, he died, to be succeeded by his flamboyant but unstable eldest son, Edward VIII.

Documents 6e. Letter from Chamberlain to Baldwin, 6 January 1935

We have our own plans, which are less spectacular [than Lloyd George's], but will probably work. L.G. will never support the National Government except on his own terms. ... [I] would not refuse to accept L.G.'s support, if offered with a single mind (!) but ... will in no circumstances sit in a Cabinet with him.

6f. Diary of A.J. Sylvester, secretary to Lloyd George, 25 March 1935

In the train [Lloyd George] told me that he now knew what this lot [the National government] was after. 'They simply want to get me to join the Government, on the promise that they will adopt my plans. They   immediately have an election and then, having been returned for five years with my assistance, politely tell me to go to Hell. But ... they will find that I have conditions. I do not want to go into the Government. ... all I am concerned about is to get my proposals adopted and out into practice. If this necessitates my taking office, I will take office, but I am not going to be tricked into a sham affair. If they won't accept my proposals I will smash them.'

Edward's behaviour was soon causing the premier some anxiety. Meanwhile, Hoare, who had the support of the newspaper magnate Lord Beaverbrook, was threatening to create all kinds of problems for the government if he was not reappointed to the cabinet (he eventually returned as First Lord of the Admiralty in June 1936). Then Thomas was found guilty of revealing budget secrets to friends who had made money betting on the contents of the budget, and forced to resign from the cabinet and leave public life. Baldwin, who was approaching 70 and increasingly deaf and jaded, seems to have had a nervous breakdown: at any rate, he went to France for three months that summer to recuperate. The high hopes which had attended the government less than a year earlier seemed shattered.

The restoration of Baldwin's fortunes came from an unlikely source. Edward VIII was a veteran seducer of other men's wives. Among the upper classes such practices were not taken too seriously so long as they did not become common knowledge or threaten public scandal. However, Edward had now become closely attached to Wallis Simpson, a married woman who was currently in the death-throes of her second marriage, her first also having ended in divorce. To make matters worse, she was an American. The cabinet, and the Labour leadership, agreed that there could be no question of Edward's marrying Simpson if he was to remain King. It seems likely that the King's pro-German sympathies were already proving an embarrassment and that, therefore, the government would be glad to be rid of him, but the extent to which he was actively conspired against remains controversial. In any event, he insisted that he wanted to marry her, and so was faced with a bleak choice. Finally, on 10 December, he announced his abdication, to be succeeded by his younger brother, who became King George VI.

Baldwin had always been at his best when faced with a constitutional crisis, as in 1926 or 1931; and he handled the abdication very well. Conversely, Churchill, who had just started to open links with other critics of the government's foreign policy, made the mistake of backing Edward, and found his credibility seriously impaired as a result. The way was now clear for Baldwin to retire in a blaze of glory. Very few modern British premiers have left office at just the time of their choosing. Baldwin was different. He stayed on until the coronation of the new King in May 1937 and then retired, at the age of 70. He was succeeded, at last, by Chamberlain, only two years his junior but with an altogether more energetic approach.

The National Government under Chamberlain, 1937-40

Chamberlain had wanted to be leader of the party, and Prime Minister, for

Baldwin (foreground) at his best: the abdication crisis. The caption to this Punch *cartoon in 1936 by Partridge reads: The Prime Minister. 'All the peoples of your Empire, Sir, sympathise with you most deeply; but they all know - as you yourself must - that the throne is greater than the man.'*

some time. He seems to have had hopes of succeeding Baldwin in the early part of 1931, but had been thwarted by the latter's unexpected sticking power in the face of press and party criticism. The formation of the National government had further hindered his progress, since it had secured Baldwin's position and subordinated both men to MacDonald. Even in 1936, when it had looked as though Baldwin could not have much longer to go, the leader had rallied and then hung on for the best part of a further year. None of this was likely to have made the already impatient Chamberlain any more easy-going.

Chamberlain, with a Birmingham family business background, came into the premiership determined to ensure that the economic recovery continued; determined to ensure the prosperity of private enterprise and the avoidance of 'socialistic' experiments; determined, once and for all, to sort out Britain's overseas responsibilities; and determined, in particular, to reach a new settlement with Germany in Europe. He started briskly. MacDonald was an ageing and embarrassing relic. He was dropped. So were others. Overall, the average age of the new cabinet, at 52, was more than three years lower than that of its predecessor: six of the 21 ministers were in their forties, and two in their thirties.

In domestic policy there were no major new departures, but rather a continuation of the basic ethos of earlier National governments. As Chancellor, Chamberlain had always been keen that reforms should be affordable. The emphasis remained on keeping government very largely out of industry. The most significant exception to this was rearmament, which had begun in 1935 and which was now being pushed ahead, albeit not quickly enough for the government's critics. When the economy moved into recession in the later part of 1937 - largely due to a renewed downturn in the USA - it was rearmament which helped to pull things round. Otherwise, the government's continued attempts, which had begun seriously with the second Labour government, to rationalise industry and particularly the old staple industries - coal, steel, shipbuilding and textiles. Legislation aiming to help agriculture continued to be passed. And a Holidays with Pay Act was passed in 1938, giving many workers the right, for the first time, to enjoy a week's paid leave a year.

Chamberlain's past record suggested that he was happiest in the realm of domestic affairs. However, he had taken an increasing interest in foreign policy during the 1930s, and he had formed very firm views that the appeasement of Germany was the way to secure a lasting peace. (These policies are discussed in detail in Chapter 9.) The key points to make here are that, up to the Munich crisis of September-October 1938, he had the overwhelming support of his ministerial colleagues and National MPs; even the resignation of Eden (over policy towards Italy) in March 1938 was fairly easily overcome, particularly as he was succeeded by Lord Halifax, who was trusted very widely both inside and beyond the party. After

Munich, however, Chamberlain became increasingly isolated within his own cabinet, and, crucially, Halifax began to doubt seriously whether appeasement remained the appropriate policy. Even so, there can be little doubt that, had not the outbreak of war intervened in September 1939, the National government, under Chamberlain, would have won a further term of office at the next election, since Labour continued to be divided and, to some extent at least, discredited during the later 1930s.

That election, which could have been expected in 1939 or early 1940, never took place because Chamberlain was finally prevailed upon to abandon appeasement and declare war on Germany following that country's invasion of Poland. On the outbreak of war, a reluctant Chamberlain suggested the possibility of a coalition to Labour's leaders, but must have known that they would refuse - indeed, he would probably not have made the offer had he expected them to accept. The main change was that Churchill was brought back to be First Lord of the Admiralty. The war began quietly for Britain: indeed, the period down to spring 1940 was christened the 'Phoney War'. There were no significant military or naval engagements for the British; nor did the expected aerial bombardment of the British mainland materialise. In early April 1940 Chamberlain was unable to restrain himself from publicly commenting that Hitler had 'missed the bus'.

However, Hitler's problems with public transport were soon solved. The British decided to mine Norwegian waters, so the Germans decided to invade Denmark and Norway. The latter plan went ahead with complete and shattering success. Belated British attempts to help the Norwegians against the invaders were disastrous. Britain had suffered a significant and humiliating defeat. In the face of this disaster, feeling against the government, and against Chamberlain, grew. The House of Commons debated the Norway campaign on 7 and 8 May 1940. Encouraged by signs of Conservative hostility towards Chamberlain, Labour put down a motion of censure on the government's handling of the affair. Chamberlain won the vote, but with a much-reduced majority of 81; 41 Conservatives voted with Labour and between 60 and 80 abstained.

Chamberlain's initial reaction was to try to stay on. But he had become too divisive a figure to start trying to charm potential allies at this late stage. There was strong feeling against him among a large minority of tories, although still much sympathy from many in the party. In addition, it seemed that a coalition must now come, and there was no way that Labour would serve under Chamberlain, whose whole career had been punctuated by sneers at Labour and its beliefs. Labour would probably have preferred his successor to be Halifax, who, although an hereditary peer, had a reputation as being on the liberal wing of the Conservative party. However, both Churchill (who was not under-ambitious) and Halifax felt that Churchill was the person for the job, and he took over on 10 May. In his five-man war cabinet were three tories - himself, Halifax and Chamberlain (as Lord President) - and two Labourites - the party leader, Attlee, and his deputy, Arthur Greenwood. The Phoney War was over, and so, too, was a whole era of British politics.

Conclusion

The National government had come to power in a mixture of confusion and glory in 1931. It left office, eight and a half years later, in ignominy. For years afterwards they remained a byword for incompetence and inaction. Yet such a verdict is not altogether fair. The governments faced massive challenges; and in many cases they faced them rather well. The economy grew impressively, although not sufficiently to wipe out high levels of unemployment in many parts of the country. The threat of political extremism was neutered far more easily than in most liberal democracies, and parliamentary government continued. And, whatever the undoubted failings of their foreign policies, they did bring Britain united into war in 1939 reasonably well-prepared to fight what seemed likely - unless it was lost - to be a long and difficult war. This is not to offer a whitewash. They were slow to see the need for specific regional policies to help the depressed areas, and, when they did act, it was weakly and for, arguably, narrowly political reasons. The debate over appeasement goes on and on, but some recent work suggests, as will be seen in Chapter 9, that more could have been done to stop Hitler earlier (although this view is strongly contested by many other historians). Whatever their failings, the National governments dominated British politics in the 1930s because they were the best thing on offer. They were by no means as incompetent as many people have suggested.

Questions to Consider
- Was the National government the logical outcome of British political developments since the war?
- Did the Labour party deserve to lose so heavily at the 1931 election?
- How credible would it have been after 1931 to argue that Labour would never again be a united party?
- What were the main features of the National governments' political strategy?
- Why did a 'safety first' strategy lead to electoral success for the National government in 1935 when it had led to defeat for the Conservatives in 1929?
- Why did no viable alternative to the National governments emerge before 1940?
- How far can the dominance of the National governments in the 1930s be explained by good luck?

7 Social Change

Introduction

During the nineteenth century, British society had been subjected to some periods of real stress and strain. While there had been a calming of social tensions between the 1850s and the 1880s, new tensions had then begun to arise, and at some points during the First World War social relations appeared to be stretched almost to breaking point. It was in this sort of context that other countries moved towards political extremism and authoritarian regimes of one kind or another, with Russia being taken over by the Bolsheviks in 1917 and Italy by the Fascists in 1922, for example. Yet somehow Britain managed to avoid these extremes, and in 1939 its government was able to take it into another war very largely united behind the national cause. This chapter will look at the main developments in British society during the period between 1916 and 1940.

The Changing Population

As stated in Chapter 2, Britain's population had grown massively during the period between the censuses of 1801 and 1911. The pace of growth, admittedly, had slowed in the period after 1851, but the population was still rising at over one per cent per year during the decade 1901-11. By the latter year, the population stood at 40.8 million.

The population continued to grow between 1911 and the outbreak of the Second World War. But it did not do so at anything like the rate that had characterised the long nineteenth century (see Tables 7.1 and 7.2).

Table 7.1 Population of England, Wales, Scotland and Britain, 1901-51 (000)

Year	England	Wales	Scotland	Britain
1901	30,515	2,013	4,472	37,000
1911	33,650	2,421	4,761	40,832
1921	35,230	2,656	4,882	42,768
1931	37,359	2,593	4,843	44,795
1939	38,995	2,465	5,007	46,467
1951	41,159	2,599	5,096	48,854

Table 7.2 Increase or Decrease (-) in Population, 1901-51 (% per year)

Period	England	Wales	Scotland	Britain
1901-11	0.98	1.86	0.63	1.04
1911-21	0.45	0.91	0.25	0.47
1921-31	0.60	-0.24	-0.08	0.47
1931-39	0.53	-0.62	0.41	0.47
1939-51	0.46	0.45	0.15	0.43

How can we account for this significant decline in the rate of population increase?

- The First World War led to the death of about 700,000 British men, while separation of men serving in the forces from their wives meant that around 600,000 births which would otherwise have taken place did not occur, leading to an estimated population deficit, due to the war, of around 1.3 million.

- These effects were offset, to a certain extent, however, by a healthier population due to full employment and hence higher incomes in wartime, and by the rise in real incomes overall even in the context of high unemployment between the wars. This, in turn, meant that death rates and rates of infant mortality fell.

- But the often difficult economic conditions of the period clearly contributed towards keeping the population down, in keeping death and infant mortality rates higher than they might otherwise have been, in urging people to delay marriage, and in discouraging people from having children.

- The birth rate, which had been falling especially among middle-class families before the First World War, now fell in all social groups. This was largely voluntary: by the 1930s it was estimated that around two-thirds of married couples were using artificial contraceptives, such as condoms.

- One theory suggests that this desire for smaller families came because men and women had been members of large families, and could thus see that opportunities for children were greater the smaller the family.

The decline in the rate of increase led to fears that the overall profile of the population would become much older, and that, ultimately, the population would begin to decline. Pessimism held sway for much of the inter-war period on this score. In 1938, the Registrars-General predicted that the population would have fallen to 45.9 million by 1971. The pressure group, Political and Economic Planning, suggested a population of between 32 and 37 million by 1989. These predictions were not borne out: the actual population in both 1971 and 1991 was around 53.9 million.

The trend towards urbanisation continued. In 1911 there were 39 towns or cities with populations of at least 100,000; by 1951 there were 59. Between the censuses of 1911 and 1931, the populations of certain major urban centres rose significantly (see Table 7.3). While some of this was due to the extension of city boundaries, a lot was to do with people moving into these large cities. The process of suburbanisation, which had begun in the previous century, continued, but it was only in the period of the Second World War and after that this began to mean absolute falls in the populations of most cities in Britain.

Table 7.3 Population of Various Cities, 1911 and 1931 (000)

	1911	1931	% increase
Greater London	7,256	8,216	13.2
Birmingham	526	1,003	90.6
Bristol	357	397	11.2
Cardiff	182	224	23.1
Coventry	106	167	57.5
Glasgow	784	1,088	38.8
Leeds	446	483	8.3
Liverpool	746	856	14.7
Manchester	714	766	7.3
Newcastle	267	283	6.0
Sheffield	455	512	12.5
BRITAIN	40,832	44,795	9.7

A Healthier Nation?

To some extent, as stated earlier, the stabilisation of the population was due to improvements in the nation's health. A number of indicators suggest that Britain was becoming healthier during the period.

- The death rate fell. Having stood at 14.7 per 1,000 in 1906-10, it was 12.5 in 1936-40.
- Infant mortality rates fell: whereas 105 out of every 1,000 babies born in 1910 had died before reaching their first birthday, this fell to 80 in 1920, 60 in 1930 and 56 in 1940.
- The rate of maternal mortality fell. In England and Wales in 1914 it had been around 4 per 1,000 live births; by 1939 it stood at 2.5.
- Life expectancy rose. A one-year old male in England or Wales could expect to live to the age of 51.5 in 1910-12; by 1930-2 this had risen to 58.7 (the corresponding figures for females were 55.4 and 62.9).

Too much should not be read into these figures, however. For one thing, some of the improvements mentioned earlier were a long time coming. In particular, the rate of maternal mortality remained stubbornly high for a long time. The 1914 figure had not been improved upon by 1934: indeed, in some areas, such as South Wales, it actually rose between the mid-1920s and the mid-1930s. Second, these average figures mask a whole range of inequalities. Social class remained a strong determinant of health.

Throughout the inter-war period, the child of an unskilled working-class father was more than twice as likely to die before reaching its first birthday as the offspring of a member of the middle or upper classes. Another, partly linked, factor was location: some parts of Britain were much healthier than others. In the late 1920s a child born in Wigan was almost twice as likely to die before its first birthday as one born in prosperous Hampstead. Gender was another divider. Despite high rates of maternal mortality, death rates among men remained significantly higher than those among women: 12.7 per 1,000 as opposed to 11.4 per 1,000 in 1931-5, for example.

Allowing for these differences, it does seem that, overall, there was some improvement in health during the period. Why was this?

- New drugs and treatments were introduced, particularly in the 1930s. The conquest of many diseases began; penicillin was in use from 1936 onwards; and there were improvements in surgical techniques.

- Knowledge about nutrition improved, and the price of food relative to wages fell significantly.

- There were some improvements in public health, with better systems of refuse collection in many parts of the country.

- Improvements in health services did take place, but largely independently of government: in some areas health authorities tried hard to improve their services. The stricter regulation of midwives from the mid-1930s, for example, probably contributed to the reduction in maternal mortality rates.

- On the whole, however, government policy seems to have played, at best, only a small part in effecting improvements. Expenditure was subjected to severe downward pressures, and there were few major initiatives during the period. There was no attempt to create a national health service.

Whatever the improvements, however, the inter-war record began to look all the more indifferent when contrasted with the very considerable advances that were to be made during and after the Second World War, when full employment, further scientific discoveries and a more forward policy on the part of government (particularly in creating the National Health Service and improving social services generally) led to much more significant improvements.

Class: Continuity and Change

'England is the most class-ridden nation under the sun,' wrote the author George Orwell in 1941. And, while there were differences between the classes, there were almost as many divisions within each class.

The upper class was the smallest of all, numbered in the thousands rather than the millions. Even here, there were divisions. On the one hand was the aristocracy and its poor cousin, the gentry. At the apex of such families were the great landowners, who had great fortunes, power and prestige. However, their grip on power was easing somewhat: such families were less well-represented in inter-war governments, for example, than they had been before 1914. Many of them sold their land, or at least some of it: between 1918 and 1921 a quarter of the land in England changed hands. For various reasons, many landowners were selling out to their tenant farmers, in order to make their assets more liquid. The other side of what might be called the upper class was made up of the very rich. The most extreme example of this was the shipowner, Sir John Ellerman, who left £33 million in his will in 1933. There was some tension between the rich and the landed, and a good deal of snobbery from the latter towards the former.

The remainder of the population could be divided, crudely, into the middle and working classes, in a proportion of about one to three. In rough terms, they can be split between those who did manual work, or got their hands dirty, and those who did not. The middle classes were usually better off, salaried rather than waged, less likely to suffer unemployment, able to afford better education and health care, and with an occupational pension to look forward to at the end of their working life. Their houses would be bigger, and it would not be unusual to find them making use of at least one living-out servant.

The working classes were generally much less well provided-for: typical images of working-class life from the literature of the period, such as Walter Greenwood's *Love on the Dole* (1933), presented a view of life as one always under threat from ill health, unemployment and poverty.

But there were also significant divisions *within* the middle and working classes. The description 'middle class', for example, covered a vast range of incomes and lifestyles. Even within the same profession, incomes could vary massively, while there were divisions between the professional middle classes, such as doctors and lawyers, and the lower middle classes such as bank clerks and lower civil servants. To generalise too far, then, about 'the experience of the middle class' would be misleading.

So too, of course, would it be to talk of the working class as a single united entity. The working classes made up about 75 per cent of the population during this period. So, not surprisingly, it is difficult to generalise. On the whole, the industrial working class fared better in this period than the agricultural (the latter, for example, usually received lower wages, suffered the problems of seasonal employment, and could not claim unemployment benefit). Industrial workers producing for the home market fared better than those producing for export. This differential applied even in single industries, for example, in coalmining wages and conditions were much better in Yorkshire and Nottinghamshire than they were in South Wales. There was a great deal of snobbery within the working class, too:

the 'respectable' working class, more likely to spend its time reading, or going to chapel or church, looked down upon the 'roughs' who were keener to go to the pub, while the latter looked down on the former as being too straightlaced and unable to enjoy themselves. Skilled workers protected their position jealously against the unskilled in industries like engineering.

In so far as one can sense a balance of interests between the middle and working classes in the period under discussion, one would have to say that the period up to 1920 or 1921 was one when the working class, albeit briefly, was in the pole position. Government, fearful of revolution or at least massive social dislocation after the war, was eager to pursue a range of social policies which aided the working class, even if this meant high taxes which hit the middle and upper classes particularly hard. However, with the end of the post-war boom and increasing evidence of middle-class discontent, government turned the other way and tried to cut back on social policies, in order to reduce expenditure and so taxation. Although trade unions, which had grown massively during the war, tried to resist, they were unable to do so to any great effect, and the defeat of the General Strike in 1926 merely came as a confirmation of a series of defeats for the unions since the mining and engineering lockouts of 1921 and 1922 respectively.

Even so, it would be wrong to portray the inter-war years as ones of unremitting gloom for the working classes. To a large extent, working-class experience varied according to the type of industry, or, within each industry, the type of firm for which one worked, or the state of the economic cycle, and so on. The unemployed worker in South Wales in the 1930s was, undoubtedly, having a grim time, desperately trying to make ends meet and to maintain a semblance of self-respect. But for workers in the South-east and the Midlands it was often a different story, with labour in short supply and wages buoyant.

Overall, then, the British social structure showed evidence of both continuity and change between the wars.

Gender: More Equality for Women?

Superficially, the inter-war years were a time of major gains for women. First, there were improvements in their legal position. In 1919, the Sex Disqualification (Removal) Act lifted restrictions on women entering the professions (other than the clergy). The divorce laws were relaxed in 1923 and 1937, although the number of divorces remained relatively low before the end of the Second World War.

There were improvements in their political rights, too. In 1918, women over 30 who themselves, or whose husbands, qualified for the local government franchise (as householders) were given the vote in parliamentary elections, and in 1928 the parliamentary franchise was given to all women over the age of 21. As from 1918, women were allowed to sit as Members of Parliament, the first woman to take her seat being the Conservative, Lady Astor, in 1919. The first woman cabinet minister, Margaret Bondfield, was appointed in 1929.

Third, the use of artificial means of contraception spread rapidly during the inter-war period, so helping the reduction in family size that was already underway. Condoms, first seen by many British men while in the Army, as a means of preventing them from catching sexually transmitted diseases, now spread beyond the middle-class constituency and into pretty general use.

Fourth, maternal mortality rates finally began to fall in the mid-1930s. When combined with the increasing limitation of family size, this meant that women were having fewer pregnancies, and that, at least late in the period, those pregnancies that women were experiencing were becoming safer.

Finally, technology appeared to many to be improving women's lot. As more and more homes were wired for electricity, and living standards generally rose, so more and more women were able to make use of labour-saving devices, such as washing machines and vacuum cleaners. In theory, at least, this might have allowed women more time to do things other than household chores, and perhaps to break into the labour market.

But too much can be made of all this. The First World War had seen many women move into the paid labour market, or else move from the drudgery of domestic service into more rewarding work. But these gains were not maintained after the war. Ironically, in the same year that sex disqualifications were being removed from the professions, women in industry were being combed out at a startling rate as men returned to the factories from the Army. The 1931 census was to show as many women in domestic service as there had been in 1911.

Political rights were granted somewhat grudgingly - the extension of the franchise in 1918 was hardly spectacular where women were concerned, and they had to wait another decade to get the vote on equal terms with men. Women MPs remained scarce: the peak figure was 15 (out of 615 MPs) in 1931. Bondfield was to prove to be the first and last woman cabinet minister before 1945. Even such women MPs as there were tended to be pigeonholed, being expected to talk mainly about 'women's' issues such as health and education.

And, given prevailing ideologies that 'a woman's place was in the home', new consumer durables might not mean more time for women to do other things, but rather, the expectation that they would, with the aid of new technologies, spend the same amount of time doing household chores to a higher standard than previously.

What did not change very much, in short, was the prevailing ideology of gender. While there were parts of Britain (most notably textile areas like

Lancashire) where it was expected that married women would work, marriage often acted as a bar to employment. This was sometimes literally the case - in teaching, and many clerical jobs, for example, it was the norm for a woman to leave her job on marriage. The ideology of 'separate spheres' returned with force after a temporary suspension during the First World War. The sphere of the man was that of work, the public sphere. That of women was the private sphere of home and family. 'Traditional' gender roles were to remain well-embedded up to and beyond the Second World War.

Education: A Better Educated Nation?

Education was not a major priority for government in the First World War. When 1916 dawned the minister in charge was Arthur Henderson, who was in the cabinet not for his knowledge of, or particular interest in, the subject, but because it was a post he could be given where there was not too much work to distract him from acting in effect as the government's adviser on labour issues. Although there were to be brief flurries of activity, this lack of serious attention was to characterise education policy during the inter-war period.

It did not seem that way at first. The nineteenth-century education system had been mainly concerned with giving people a basic level of literacy and numeracy, and with social control - that is, trying to ensure that people became respectful of their betters and of the existing social order. The 1918 'Fisher' Education Act, named after the Coalition Liberal minister responsible, seemed to move away from such a limited view. It provided for a number of changes. The school-leaving age was raised from 12 to 14. After 14, most young people would go to work, but also attend 'continuation schools' one day a week until they were 16, to further improve their skills. Fisher also stressed that, as soon as possible, the leaving age would be raised to 15. The Act also increased state subsidies to local education authorities.

Such moves seemed radical. However, the Act did nothing about the curriculum, church schools, or the independent sector. Universities remained wholly outside its ambit. Much of the impetus behind continuation schools was about social control, not improving young workers' skills; in any case, employers disliked having to pay workers for a day spent at school every week. When it came to implementing the Act, many local authorities were reluctant, and acted slowly. In any case, the spending cuts suggested by the Geddes Committee (see page 24) soon put paid to continuation schools, and the raising of the leaving age to 15 was postponed indefinitely.

In many ways Geddes set the tone for the rest of the inter-war period. The children of social elites continued to be educated in independent schools, outside the state sector. Secondary education remained something of a privilege, with fees being charged for all but the poorest of students. Universities, of which there were only a handful, catered essentially for the better off, and there was no aspiration towards mass access to higher education. Education proved to be a less sensitive budget than others, and so was more easily cut or restricted.

There were occasional attempts at change. Sir Charles Trevelyan, Education minister in the second Labour government, did introduce a bill to increase the age to 15, but this was damaged by Catholic backbenchers anxious that not enough money would be given to that church's schools to compensate for the larger numbers that would result, and destroyed by the House of Lords. Things then got even worse when the National government's economy package saw swingeing cuts in education spending.

The 1930s saw little real change. As the economic situation eased, there was a little more money, but the only at all dramatic development was the passing of an Act in 1936 to raise the leaving age to 15 from 1 September 1939. Unfortunately, that was the day that Hitler decided to invade Poland, and so the measure was postponed, only finally to be adopted in 1947.

By 1940 the education system had made little real progress from 1916. There were still obstacles to central control from local authorities, and from religious denominations jealous of their rights over 'their' schools. The curriculum remained rather backward-looking; in particular, science and technology were almost universally weak, whether in the state or independent school sector, or in the universities. Lack of state control over the independent schools and universities made for a patchwork system with little co-ordination.

This is not to say that there were no improvements. Pupil to teacher ratios gradually fell during the 1930s. There was some limited expansion of university and secondary education in the later 1930s. And all children were, at least, receiving an elementary education until they were 14. In addition, schooling was not the only source of education: the press, cheap books, and adult education all played their part.

Nevertheless, it was to be left to the governments of the Second World War and after to push matters forward in this field: the inter-war period left a great deal to be done in the field of education.

Religion: A Secularising Society?

During the nineteenth century Britain had liked to see itself as a Christian country. The monarch was head of the Established Church, the Church of England; those who, for whatever reason, were not Anglicans could find solace with the Nonconformist churches, such as the Methodists, Congregationalists or Baptists, or with the Roman Catholic Church (the latter catering mainly, though not exclusively, for Irish immigrants and their descendants). Many politicians made no secret of their faith:

Gladstone, for example, had paraded his godliness.

Many historians have argued that, since the nineteenth-century peak in religious observance, Christianity has become marginalised, and that Britain has moved towards being a secular, or non-religious, country. While there are those who would dispute this thesis, there seems little doubt that Christianity has moved from the centre of the stage. The inter-war period certainly saw at best a levelling off and at worst a decline in religious observance for the Anglican and Nonconformist churches (see Table 7.4). At best, the figures were stable, which was hardly encouraging given that the population was rising. The Nonconformists were clearly faring worst. The one denomination which seemed to be continuing its advance was the Roman Catholic Church. Membership here rose steadily throughout this period, from 2.2 million in 1910 to 2.5 million in 1920, 2.8 million in 1930 and 3.0 million in 1940, although it should be noted that this figure was boosted somewhat by continuing immigration from Ireland, and that no one would claim that all of these Catholics were active in their religious observance.

Table 7.4 Membership of Selected Churches, 1914-1939 (000)

	1914	1929	1939
Church of England	2,226	2,304	2,245
Church of Scotland plus United Free Church of Scotland	1,230	1,284	1,285
Methodists	827	840	801
Baptists	412	403	381
Congregationalists	489	490	456
Welsh Presbyterians	185	186	177

Why were the churches, taken as a whole, losing ground during this period? A number of ideas have been put forward, some more convincing than others:

- During the nineteenth century there had been little else to do on a Sunday but go to church, but the leisure revolution of the inter-war period (see overleaf) meant that there were now alternatives.

- There was a growth in doubt regarding the key canons of religious faith: theories of evolution challenged the idea that God had created the Earth in seven days, for example. Such doubts were intensified as scientific discovery proceeded apace.

- The social service functions of the churches, which had done so much to bind people to them in the nineteenth century, went into decline, and were taken over by the State.

- The political role of the churches declined as other pressure groups came to the centre of the stage (for example, trade unions within the Labour party).

● Religion: A Secularising Society?

- Church-going habits were disrupted, first by the First World War, and then by the extensive rehousing that went on during the inter-war period.

- Moves towards church unity, most marked in the Methodist churches where what had been five separate sects in 1900 had eventually merged as one by 1933, produced a certain blandness which made some people disillusioned.

- In attempting to appear 'modern' and 'relevant', the churches - or some of them - moved away from the more glamorous, miraculous side of their teaching and so reduced their members' enthusiasm (in support of this argument it can be stated that the Catholic Church, which did not follow this path, fared best).

All the same, we have to be careful not to 'over-explain' the 'decline', as *absolute* falls in membership were only to become commonplace during the post-war period. And, in a broader sense, religion continued to be important to inter-war Britain. It determined social behaviour patterns, at least indirectly. It was a leading influence on politicians as diverse as Baldwin and Henderson. Divorce remained difficult to obtain, despite some liberalisation, and socially stigmatised. The Sabbath was still rigorously observed in many parts of Britain, especially Wales and Scotland; trading restrictions were tight, and during the late 1920s and early 1930s there was an almighty row about whether parks and cinemas should be open on Sunday or not. The British might have been less conscientious in their church attendance, but they could not seriously pretend that they were living in a secular society.

Leisure: A More Leisured Society?

One factor which damaged church attendance was the rise of alternative leisure activities. This is not to say that leisure opportunities were absent before 1914, of course. The pub, sport, and music hall had all been available to, and widely used by, the working classes. More 'respectable' recreations, such as reading, hobbies, and walking had also been popular. However, the inter-war period saw leisure develop in new ways. The preconditions for this were all met: working hours fell; most people became better off as real wages increased; and, as a result, both private and public sector provision of leisure grew significantly.

The pub continued to be important for many working-class men. However, its grip was weakening somewhat. In 1900, around 11 per cent of household expenditure was going on drink; by 1935, this had fallen to about 7 per cent. New, more restrictive opening hours (including afternoon closing) brought in during the First World War were to remain in force until the 1980s. Beer became weaker. And the character of pubs began to change. Where they had once been male-only preserves, and of a very basic nature, they began, particularly during the 1930s, to welcome couples (although single women were still often frowned upon). Today, many of Britain's large cities are ringed by 1930s suburban pubs, huge in size, plush by the standards of the time, and with large car parks, designed much more than ever before for a male and female clientelle. Not all men, it has to be said, welcomed the new mixed nature of pubs: one response was to set up working-men's clubs, from which women were barred.

Sport remained popular. At the level of spectator sport, the inter-war years saw massive interest, particularly in soccer, where crowds reached

Upper middle-class young people at play

- Leisure: A More Leisured Society?   **69**

unprecedented levels: it was estimated that anything up to 200,000 people watched the first Wembley FA Cup Final in 1923. Rugby and cricket also remained popular. New sports, like speedway, were introduced with some success. Horseracing was joined by greyhounds as a sport for gamblers: indeed, gambling was a central part of working-class culture, no mean feat given that off-course betting remained, in theory at least, illegal. Sporting participation also seems to have increased, as local authorities provided more playing fields, swimming baths, and so on.

The period saw the decline of the old music hall but the very significant advance of the cinema. The first commercial film-show in Britain had been in 1896; by 1916, millions of people a week were going to the cinema to see silent films. The upward trend continued pretty well unabated throughout the inter-war period. American films became especially popular, to such an extent that, in 1927, the government passed legislation which tried to restrict the number of foreign films shown. The first sound film, *The Jazz Singer*, was shown in 1930. By 1934 there were over 4,000 cinemas in Britain, and average weekly attendances were around 18.5 million, rising to 20 million by 1939. Film stars became icons. However, it should be remembered that there were clear differences between rural and urban areas, for the latter were far better provided for than the former.

Another recreation that relied on 'new technology' was radio. The British Broadcasting Company, set up in 1923, was nationalised (as the British Broadcasting Corporation) in 1926. Under its director-general, John Reith, it took a serious, and not infrequently sombre, view of its role, but it was popular, none the less, partly because Reith was not always able to get his own way. From being virtually unheard of at the end of the First World War, radio became so widespread that, by 1939, three-quarters of households had a receiver. Television was also invented during the period, and broadcasts began to a few thousand households in the south of England in 1936, but these were suspended on the outbreak of war: overwhelmingly, this was a radio age.

Reading also played a significant part in people's leisure activities. The habit of newspaper reading, already well-entrenched within the middle class and the upper echelons of the working classes before 1914, now became almost universal. In the 1930s, popular newspapers like the *Daily Express* and the *Daily Herald* vied with each other for readers in often brutal circulation wars. Heavyweight quality papers like *The Times* and the *Daily Telegraph* were available to those who wanted a fuller and less sensational read. While the development of a national press had begun long before our period, it was between the wars that the national press finally took the lead: local and regional papers lost market share dramatically. Here, as with cinema and radio, local diversity was being reduced. Magazines thrived, too, not least women's magazines. The 1930s

Leisure: A More Leisured Society? ●

also saw the development of the cheap book. Particularly important here were Penguin Books, which provided a paperback book, be it a novel, a travel book or a political 'Penguin Special' for the price of a packet of cigarettes. When to this is added the continuing development of libraries run by local authorities, it can be seen that the British people had more material available to read than ever before,

Other leisure pursuits which developed included motoring and holidays. While cars remained too expensive for most members of the working classes, there was a big increase in middle-class car ownership. What had been the preserve of the rich before the First World War now came within the grasp of many more ordinary people. In 1914 there had been 132,000 private cars in use: by 1928 this had risen to 1,944,000. Freight traffic on the roads also increased dramatically. Indeed, traffic began to be such a problem that, in 1934, the Minister of Transport, Leslie Hore-Belisha, was forced to introduce the 30 miles per hour speed limit in built-up areas and the zebra crossing, which remains part of motoring - and walking - to this day.

The pursuit of holidaying also increased in popularity as people found they had more time and money. The Holidays with Pay Act, 1938, provided for a week's paid holiday to certain categories of workers. Partly as a result of this, the number entitled to a week's paid leave rose from 1 million in 1920 and 4 million in 1937 to 11 million in 1939. By that time there were around 200 holiday camps in Britain; Billy Butlin had set up his first camp at Skegness in 1937. Camping, and staying at boarding houses in resorts like Blackpool and Scarborough, were also popular pursuits. It was still true to say, though, that it was only the wealthy who could afford to holiday abroad.

Finally, hobbies continued to flourish. Many of these were home-based, further reinforcing the view that, as people became better off and housing conditions improved, they were readier to stay at home when not at work. Second, a strong gender differential continued. Women and men were, on the whole, likely to pursue hobbies in their own 'sphere': that is to say, women would knit, or crochet, or embroider, while men decorated, or put up shelves, or bred pigeons.

By 1939, then, Britain was a somewhat more leisured society than it had been a quarter of a century earlier. Some aspects of that leisure were now more private and domestic; others were clearly more 'national', helping to pull together the people's experiences as never before. However, there remained very significant developments in the future, such as the development of mass car ownership, television and foreign holidays. In many ways the inter-war period was as different, in leisure terms, from today as it was from the period which had preceded it.

Conclusion

British society was divided, in many ways, in this period. However, it would not do to overstate the divisions. Social conflict was never so strong as to threaten the overthrow of the political and social order. Somehow 'the system' was able to cope, against often quite daunting odds. At the same time, there were signs that older divisions, such as locality, were becoming less important as a more national culture was forged with the help of radio, cinema and the press. There was some social change, largely driven by increasing living standards, but for some - most notably women - the changes were often more apparent than real. Yet the most striking sign of the underlying unity of British society was the failure of the extremist movements, Communism and Fascism, to make more than a marginal impact, and the fact that, despite all the trials and tribulations of the early part of the Second World War, society did not fragment.

Questions to Consider
- What were the main changes in Britain's population in this period?
- How far and why did the British become healthier?
- How far was Britain a class-ridden society?
- How far and why did the position of women in society change?
- What were the main concerns in the making of education policy?
- To what extent and why did religion decline?
- What were the causes and effects of the changes in leisure patterns between the wars?

8 The Economy

Introduction

During this period the British economy faced serious challenges. The world situation was, for the most part, far from favourable. The trade cycle moved in ways which often made it difficult for Britain to sustain any kind of prosperity. Industry was undergoing a degree of restructuring, with 'old' industries losing relative importance to 'new' ones. Governments, for their part, were reluctant to get too closely involved in the workings of the economy, and tried so far as possible to let things work themselves out in accordance with free market economics. What is impressive, having said all this, is the progress that the economy *did* manage to make between 1916 and 1940.

The Trade Cycle

The basic principle of the trade cycle is very straightforward. At certain times demand for products is very high. This produces a boom, with high levels of economic activity and low levels of unemployment. At other times, the economy lacks demand. Low economic activity (recession, depression, slump) results, meaning high unemployment. The British economy between 1916 and 1940 was buffeted heavily by the economic cycle. Thus, unemployment was often high and sometimes very high. It is important to remember, though, that inter-war unemployment was not all the result of the operations of the trade cycle. As will be seen in the following section, much of it stemmed from problems in the structure of the economy. This *structural* unemployment would have been present whatever the state of the trade cycle.

The basic story of the economic cycle in this period is fairly easily told. In 1916, the war economy was operating at near full capacity. The government was spending vast sums of money on arms, ammunition, uniforms, and so on for the war effort. This was largely financed by loans (the national debt multiplied ten-fold during the war). Full employment meant increased wages; increased wages, in turn, further fuelled demand. Such was the demand for labour that there were shortages of workers, which explains why so many women entered industrial employment for the first time.

The year 1919 saw something of a 'shake-out' of workers, especially women, from industry. This, and the initial problems caused by demobilisation of the armed forces and an easing of demand with the end of the war, explains why unemployment rose during 1919. However, the economy entered a frantic post-war boom as speculators gambled that good times would go on for ever. Unemployment remained low, with the consequence, noted in Chapter 4, that the labour movement found itself with unprecedented membership and leverage. However, this, along with the rising prices and decline in the value of money associated with it, caused concern within the government and among its supporters, especially in the middle class among those living on fixed incomes.

As a result of such fears, the government decided to cool down the economy, reducing demand by cutting public spending and raising taxes and interest rates. But this came at a time when Britain's export competitors were beginning to recover. British exports were beginning to look relatively expensive, and demand for them fell. These factors, added to a natural relaxation of domestic demand, sent the economy into a tailspin from the summer of 1920. A very sharp recession saw the economy move from boom to a deep slump in the space of around six months. Unemployment rocketed (see Table 8.1) and Gross Domestic Product (GDP) fell by over 10 per cent in less than two years.

Table 8.1 Unemployment, 1913-46

Year	% of Insured Workers Unemployed	Year	% of Insured Workers Unemployed
1913	3.6	1929	10.4
1916	0.6	1930	16.1
1917	0.7	1931	21.3
1918	0.8	1932	22.1
1919	n/a	1933	19.9
1920	3.9	1934	16.7
1921	16.9	1935	15.5
1922	14.3	1936	13.1
1923	11.7	1937	10.8
1924	10.3	1938	12.9
1925	11.3	1939	9.3
1926	12.5	1940	6.0
1927	9.7	1941	2.2
1928	10.8	1946	2.5

After 1921, however, there was a slow, halting, but none the less real recovery. It would be a little optimistic, however, to argue that the years from about 1923 to 1929 saw a real boom. There was certainly nothing to compare with the boom conditions which prevailed in the United States in the same period. Unemployment, for example, never fell below one million.

Documents 8a. Liberal Party, *We Can Conquer Unemployment* (the 'Orange Book'), March 1929

We believe we can throw off the national shoulders the Old Man of the Sea of unemployment, if we have the will, and if we follow the large-scale and definite policy which we now propose. We have the men, the money, and the management; put together, these mean goods and services for the benefit of the whole nation. Let us put them together.

8b. Winston Churchill, House of Commons, 15 April 1929

The total development expenditure of the present Government during their period of office already exceeds £300,000,000, and there is a further £50,000,000 of commitments in sight. ... The point I am coming to is that for the purpose of curing unemployment the results have certainly been disappointing. They are, in fact, so meagre as to lend considerable colour to the orthodox Treasury doctrine which has been steadfastly held that, whatever might be the political or social advantages, very little additional employment and no permanent additional employment can in fact and as a general rule be created by State borrowing and State expenditure.

Only in 1927 was the 1913 level of Gross Domestic Product exceeded, although it had almost been equalled in 1925. There was little of what would today be called the 'feelgood factor', and this helps to explain why Baldwin's Conservative government lost the 1929 election. The halting nature of the economic upturn had a number of causes. These included structural weaknesses, like the overpricing of British exports, the increase in foreign competition, and the economic weakness of many of Britain's former export customers. Policy also played its part: the return to the gold standard in 1925, in particular, seems to have increased the difficulties of the export industries, although it did not cause them. Finally, the General Strike and, more particularly, the six-month mining lockout in 1926 dampened down the economy very considerably indeed.

The context of the 1929 election was one in which the Conservatives were condemned by their opponents for not turning moderately good economic prospects into tangible prosperity, rather than of deep depression. However, this soon changed into a headlong economic decline. Unemployment began to rise significantly in August 1929, although the trend had been generally upwards since 1927. The world economic crash which, to a large extent, originated in the United States but which had wider causes, then hit Britain dramatically. The jobless total rose every month between then and the start of 1931, and even then the trend remained upwards. As seen in Chapter 5, unemployment more than doubled under the second Labour government, to 2.7 million. The government was not responsible for the crisis. But it would be hard to argue that it did much to improve matters, and by the summer of 1931 it had clearly lost whatever business confidence it had ever had. The coming to power of the National government, with a clearer set of ideas on how to face the crisis, plus the departure from gold in September 1931, did stabilise the economy somewhat, and unemployment fell between then and the year's end. However, these were essentially short-term bonuses. The economy continued in the doldrums during 1932, with unemployment rising to its peak late that year.

British unemployment levels were high, but not as high or as potentially destabilising as those being experienced in Germany or the United States at the same time. And, from 1932 to 1937, there was a period of recovery ending in a cyclical boom. This was partly helped along by government policy, as will be seen later, and also by natural forces of recovery and the partial revival of the American economy.

The cycle reached a peak in mid-1937. This did not produce full employment, or anything like it: unemployment remained well above a million. But this was due to structural factors, as will be seen later. In many parts of the country, all the signs of a boom, most notably severe shortages of skilled labour, were present. In the final quarter of 1937 this cyclical boom broke, not least because of a serious slump in America. However, what could have been a deep recession was largely averted because government expenditure on rearmament was increasing at the time. This spending, and later the outbreak of war, further stimulated economic activity. By the late summer of 1940 unemployment was almost eradicated. For all the cyclical trends between 1916 and 1940, the overall cycle had turned a full revolution, from, and back to, full employment in time of war.

The Structure of the Economy

The reason unemployment remained so high in inter-war Britain even during cyclical booms was the fact that structural problems loomed so large. Before 1914, Britain's economic strength and prosperity had rested primarily on the staple industries. These were the industries of the Industrial Revolution: coal, textiles, shipbuilding and iron and steel. These industries produced for the domestic market, of course, but it was their export potential that had really enabled the British economy to prosper. In the mid-nineteenth century they had allowed Britain to become the world's leading economic power. This domination had come under severe threat, particularly from the United States and Germany, between the 1870s and 1914. However, the problems were much greater after the end of the First World War, with the result that the staples, overall, struggled (see Table 8.2):

- There was the problem of substitution: countries which had previously bought goods from Britain were often forced, by the change in British priorities towards production for the war effort, to find new suppliers. Many of these markets were then lost for good.
- Some countries began to industrialise themselves more intensively, and

as this process continued through the inter-war period so Britain lost valuable export markets.

- British exports began to look expensive. This was partly because their competitors were more efficient because they used newer plant in larger-scale enterprises, but industrial costs in Britain also remained high - and despite the onset of high levels of unemployment after 1920, labour costs (wages), especially in the heavily unionised staple industries, were difficult to cut very far.
- This problem of over-priced exports was certainly not helped, and was probably worsened, by the return to gold at the pre-war parity of 1:$4.86 in 1925.
- After a brief boom, the price of commodities fell massively and remained very low for the rest of the inter-war period. Because many of Britain's export customers were primarily commodities' producers, who used the receipts of their exports to buy British goods, this hit British exports hard.

Table 8.2 Percentage Unemployment in the Staple Industries, 1929-1938

	1929	1932	1936	1938
Coal	18.2	41.2	25.0	22.0
Cotton	14.5	31.1	15.1	27.7
Shipbuilding	23.2	59.5	30.6	21.4
Iron and Steel	19.9	48.5	29.5	24.8
Average for industries	9.9	22.9	12.5	13.3

In the largest staple, coal, there were massive problems of inefficiency, poor industrial relations and high costs. Various government efforts to resolve the problems came to little. The 1919 Sankey Commission recommended nationalisation by a narrow majority, but the government ignored it. Indeed, wartime state control was ended in April 1921, leading to a four-month lockout which ended with the miners returning to work on the employers' terms. Some relief was gained by cyclical recovery and the temporary difficulties of competitors (such as the effects of the French occupation of the German Ruhr coalfield in 1923). But the subsequent increase in competition and the return to gold in 1925 led to further difficulties. As seen in Chapter 5, the upshot of all this was the 1925 subsidy to the coal industry and the mining lockout and General Strike of 1926. These disputes, however, ended in defeat for the unions and, again, the miners went back to work on the employers' terms. The Samuel Report (March 1926) had made various recommendations about modernisation of the industry, but the owners disliked its interventionism, the miners would be satisfied with nothing short of full nationalisation, and successive governments lacked the will or the means to force through really meaningful change. Although there were some prosperous coalfields

Documents 8c. J.B. Priestley, *English Journey* **(1934)**

I had seen a lot of Englands. How many? At once, three disengaged themselves from the shifting mass. There was, first, Old England, the country of the cathedrals and minsters and manor houses and inns, of Parson and Squire; guide-book and quaint high ways and byways England. ... Then ... there is the nineteenth-century England, the industrial England of coal, iron, steel, cotton, wool, railways; of thousands of rows of little houses all alike. ... The third England ... was the new post-war England. ... America, I supposed, was its real birthplace. This is the England of arterial and by-pass roads, of filling stations and factories that look like exhibition buildings, of giant cinemas and dance-halls and cafes, bungalows with tiny garages, cocktail bars, Woolworths, motor-coaches, wireless, hiking, factory girls looking like actresses, greyhound racing and dirt tracks, swimming pools, and everything given away for cigarette coupons.

8d. 'A Derbyshire Miner's Wife', in H.L. Beales and R.S. Lambert, *Memoirs of the Unemployed* **(1934)**

My husband is a good man. ... But he is a changed man these last two years. He never complains, but I wish he would. It makes me unhappy to find him becoming quieter and quieter when I know what he must be feeling. If I had someone to talk to about my troubles I should feel better. But having to keep them to myself, as my husband does, makes everything so much the worse. We quarrel far more now than we have ever done in our lives before. We would both rather be dead than go on like this; but there is no prospect of a change if my husband does not begin to work again.

---

between the wars, such as those being newly opened up in Nottingham-shire and Kent, the exporting areas like South Wales and County Durham remained very depressed indeed, with very high levels of unemployment and deprivation right up to the Second World War.

The fortunes of the other staples were also poor, on the whole. Shipbuilding was the worst hit, with massive overcapacity and very high levels of unemployment. The story of cotton textiles, centred on Lancashire, was broadly similar. The steel industry also suffered, although at least here there were growing new opportunities offered by the development of new industries, most notably motor cars.

Such 'new' industries had been boosted by the First World War. They included, as well as the car industry, chemicals, aircraft, light engineering and artificial textiles. During the inter-war period they continued to develop. They tended not to be located in the same areas as the staples, though. The classic areas of the Industrial Revolution were largely bypassed as the new industries located closer to their markets, especially in the South-east and the Midlands. Towns like Slough and Reading became major industrial centres. Coventry became a boom town in the 1930s on the back of cars and aeroplanes.

This mismatch between the location of the old declining industries and the new more dynamic ones caused major problems. First, as stated previously, it meant that unemployment was very high in the staples' heartlands (see Table 8.3). Second, though, it also meant that there were often labour shortages in the booming areas. Finally, the making of economic policy became very difficult. For which areas should economic policy be made: those with booming new industries or those with declining old ones?

Table 8.3 Unemployment in Various Places, September 1936

	% unemployed	% unemployed for a year or more
Deptford, London	6.7	0.4
Leicester	7.4	0.8
Liverpool	25.7	5.9
Blackburn, Lancs	29.5	11.2
Crook, Co Durham	33.6	18.8
Rhondda, S Wales	44.5	28.1

The solution which governments moved towards, rather haltingly and with some reluctance, was regional policy. In the 1920s this involved crude industrial transference schemes: unemployed workers from depressed areas were given help in finding jobs in, and moving to, more prosperous areas. The results of this were unimpressive, however, and ran into the sand with the onset of the depression from 1929 onwards (since unemployment was high everywhere). However, from 1932 the regional differentials became more pronounced once again, and in 1934 the press (and many National MPs who had unexpectedly won seats in depressed areas in 1931 and hoped to keep them at the next election) began to call for something to be done. The result was the Special Areas Act of 1934. This was significant in that it was to prove a precursor of the much more active regional policies that would follow the Second World War, but it was, very largely, a cosmetic exercise. It designated four 'special' (that is, depressed) areas: South Wales, North-eastern England and West Cumberland, under one commissioner, and industrial Central Scotland (excluding Glasgow), under another. Each commissioner, though, had an annual budget of £1 million, and the projects the money could be spent on were strictly limited. At best the Act had a very marginal effect. What was really to revive the staple areas was rearmament and, later, war.

The continuing problems faced by the depressed areas suggests that the overall amount of restructuring within the British economy during the 1920s and 1930s was not so great as some historians have alleged. The staple industries remained uncomfortably central to the overall fortunes of the economy, and no government could simply have written them off, partly because the 'new' industries, in turn, were not growing all that strongly. As a percentage of the value of total net output, the new industries' share rose from 14.1 per cent in 1924 to 21 per cent in 1935. Over the same period, the share for the old industries did fall, but only

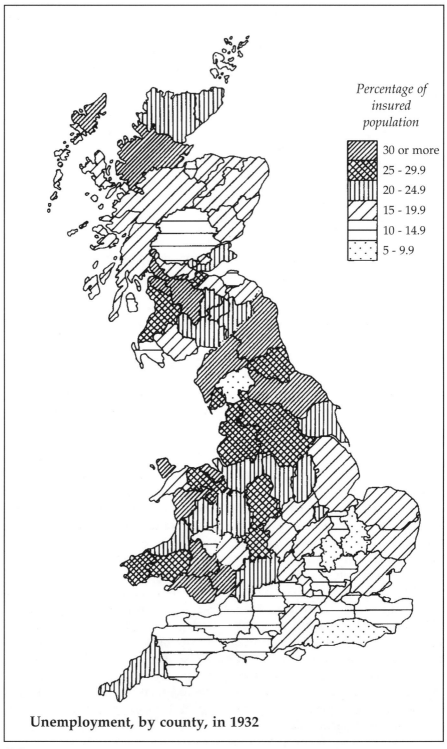

*Percentage of
insured
population*

	30 or more
	25 - 29.9
	20 - 24.9
	15 - 19.9
	10 - 14.9
	5 - 9.9

Unemployment, by county, in 1932

from 37 to 27.8 per cent. Thus, while Britain's industrial structure did evolve between 1916 and 1940, it did not change as radically as has sometimes been alleged.

Economic Policy

One of the major areas of controversy regarding inter-war British history is that surrounding economic policy. Broadly, policy in the period can be divided into three periods: from 1916 to about 1921; from 1921 until 1931; and from 1931 until 1940.

During the first of these periods, the overwhelming priority of economic policy was to provide the means for the war to be won and the transition to peace to be made. The accession of Lloyd George, supporting victory at any price, to the premiership in December 1916 was a powerful symbol of this, although in reality a start had been made under Asquith. Three aspects of policy were particularly significant. First, control over all aspects of the economy increased. Second, the government was committed, as had been its predecessor, to the financing of the war effort out of loans, rather than taxation. And, finally, the government was prepared to depart from the old orthodoxies of liberal economics such as free trade, the gold standard, and balanced budgets, if victory necessitated it. In none of these respects was there a massive change from what the Asquith Coalition had already been doing - the gold standard had been suspended, and some tariffs introduced, by 1915, while it had soon become apparent that a balanced budget was an impossibility given the levels of expenditure needed to fight a total war.

The needs of social reconstruction, electoral considerations, and fears of social upheaval on the scale being experienced by many countries on the Continent, discouraged the Coalition from moving away from interventionism once the war was over. However, it became increasingly clear during 1919 and 1920 that things could not carry on as they were: expenditure, and taxes, remained high, and there was increasing pressure for a change back to a less interventionist policy. The result was that from 1920 onwards the government began to reduce its role in the economy, for example, by stressing its intention to return to the gold standard, returning control of the coal mines to their owners, and imposing new limits on public expenditure.

During the period from 1921 until 1930, there was a much greater degree of consensus between Labour and Conservative leaders about economic policy than is usually realised (a point which should be remembered when considering party politics and election results in Chapters 4, 5 and 6). Both parties were broadly committed, when in government, to balanced budgets, the gold standard, and free trade. Both parties believed, essentially, that the only way in which to solve Britain's economic difficulties was to avoid dangerous experiments at home while trying to restore the international economy to health. The 1920s can thus be seen as an era of economic internationalism. Experiments, such as a shift towards protectionism (for the Conservatives) or nationalisation (for Labour), were largely shunned. Imperialists, like Amery, who wanted an imperial trading bloc protected by high tariffs from foreign competition, were disappointed, as were left-wing socialists, like James Maxton, who wanted nationalisation and higher taxes to pay workers a 'living wage'. Labour's economic policymakers believed firmly that socialism could only arise gradually from the successful operation of the capitalist system: to interfere too far would push down tax revenues and so reduce the scope for meaningful social reform.

The economic internationalist approach was not without its successes: progress was made in reducing German reparations' payments by the Dawes and Young Plans (1924 and 1929, respectively). Unemployment levels during the 1920s were low compared with what was to follow in the early 1930s. However, the persistence of what appeared to be unfeasibly high levels of unemployment led some critics to argue that a new way forward was needed. The Liberal economist, John Maynard Keynes, was a strong critic of many aspects of economic internationalism. He argued that the return to the gold standard in 1925 overvalued the pound and so made British exports uncompetitive; he increasingly questioned the value of a balanced budget; and by early 1931 he was calling openly for a degree of protectionism. But even though some of his ideas were taken up by the Liberal party at the 1929 election, that party remained committed, at least in theory, to the internationalism of balanced budgets, gold standard and free trade. In any case, they could not do better than 59 seats in 1929, and this was generally taken as a rejection of a more radical approach to the nation's economic ills. As for Keynes, his vigorous self-promotion and publicity-seeking in the late 1920s and early 1930s aroused considerable distrust within the political establishment.

It was the slump, which became so apparent in late 1929, which changed matters. The writing had been on the wall for free trade for some time, but recession acted as a powerful motor in pushing the nation's economic policymakers towards a new approach. The second Labour government, and Chancellor Snowden, in particular, tried hard to maintain the gold standard, balanced budget and free trade. But it was a losing battle. Attempts at international tariff truces brought meagre results. By the summer of 1930 business was almost unanimously in favour of protective tariffs, and that October the Conservatives finally came out for protection with imperial preference. Even many Liberals were now giving up on free trade, and some Labour ministers began to come towards the same conclusion, although they could do little against Snowden's resistance.

Despite the efforts of the National government, formed in August 1931, Britain was forced off gold that September, and this brought about a new approach to economic policy. The sweeping victory of the government at that October's general election paved the way for a new, more nationalist, approach to economic policy, as it was realised that international solutions were now more remote than ever (a conclusion finally driven home by the dismal failure of the London World Economic Conference of 1933). The National government remained committed to the view that there should be no massive extension of state intervention in the economy, and that the best way of promoting recovery was to create conditions in which private enterprise could flourish. However, it also adopted a number of innovations:

- It refused to try to return to gold, preferring instead to manage the exchange rate through the exchange equalisation account.
- Since sterling was no longer linked to gold, it was no longer necessary to attract foreign gold by means of high interest rates, and this meant that a 'cheap money' policy could be followed, with interest rates never varying from 2 per cent between June 1932 and August 1939.
- It introduced protection with the Import Duties Act of 1932, and followed this with a degree of imperial preference after the Ottawa agreements with the Dominions that September.
- It launched a much more interventionist period with regard to agriculture, including the establishment of produce marketing boards, and so on.
- From 1934 onwards the Special Areas Act marked a new attention to regional policy.

All of this did not add up to a great deal of hype and drama. At the side of the Soviet five year plans, Roosevelt's New Deal or the Nazi 'economic miracle', the exchange equalisation account seemed a pretty pale effort. And yet the government was able to preside over a general easing of economic difficulties to such an extent that, by about 1934, the cyclical slump was over and employment levels were rising impressively. Although unemployment remained stubbornly high in many parts of Britain, this was made less of a political problem by the maintenance of the benefits system, as seen in Chapter 6.

Of course there were many who rejected this approach. Keynes argued for huge public works programmes which would build houses and roads and get the unemployed back to work. The basic idea here was that such schemes should be paid for by loans taken out by government when the economy was in the doldrums. The expenditure would stimulate demand within the economy because, instead of existing on low levels of benefit, people would have a wage to spend. This would, in turn, lead to other people gaining work, to produce goods to cater for the demand newly created. This was the 'multiplier effect': namely, that for every job created directly by public works, others would follow. This strategy was not fully worked out until Keynes published his *General Theory* in 1936, although earlier versions of it could be seen in the Liberals' 1929 manifesto and in the Mosley Memorandum of 1930. United States President F.D. Roosevelt's 'New Deal', started in 1933, has often been cited as an example of successful Keynesian economics.

Yet these plans were shot through with drawbacks.

- They would have involved the government taking out huge loans, at a time when the burden of war debt remained a serious problem reminding policymakers of the dangers of mortgaging the future for present expenditure.
- There was also a fear that if government tried to borrow large amounts of money, interest rates would inevitably rise, killing off recovery in the private sector and plunging the country into a new depression.
- Reflation might also suck in imports and make exports less competitive, thus damaging the trade balance - and exporting areas - seriously.
- There were also administrative problems: the money would take a long time to spend, because building new roads (for example) involved a whole series of plans, inquiries, and so on.
- Many of the new roads and houses were most needed in those parts of the country that were economically vibrant, such as the Midlands and the South-east: how would building new roads to the west of London give work to unemployed miners in Cumberland or South Wales, at least without massive problems of transferring the working population from one end of the country to the other?
- The people advocating public works - Lloyd George, Keynes, Mosley and so on - were very largely discredited by the early 1930s, and not seen as honest or trustworthy.
- Foreign examples of successful Keynesian experiments were rare before the mid-1930s, and even those that have been seen as successful - such as Roosevelt's New Deal - are now seen by many historians as having had only a marginal impact (at best) on economic recovery.

More radical approaches had even less chance of being implemented. The Labour party was reeling from defeat in 1931. It did gradually piece together an economic strategy during the 1930s, based on a combination of nationalisation of industry and socialist economic planning. But the first fruits of this only came with the programme *For Socialism and Peace* (1934) and it was not until 1937, with Labour's *Immediate Programme*, that the party's economic ideas could, in any real sense, be described as being worked out. Even then, they still seemed to many people to be rather half-baked, and did little to attract much of the electorate. Mosley's Fascists lacked any real credibility as gurus of economic policymaking. Other parties, like the Liberals and the Communists, had even less to offer in this area. What finally got the depressed areas moving again was the onset of large-scale rearmament, from 1937 onwards, followed by the return to conditions of total war by mid-1940. It is a grim commentary on the period under discussion that only war appeared capable of offering an escape, for many, from unemployment and its consequent evils.

The economic policies pursued by governments between 1916 and 1940 were not, on the whole, terribly exciting. All the same, it can be said that things could have been much worse than they were, and that, broadly speaking, inter-war governments did a great deal to ensure that the British economic experience was nowhere near as traumatic as that in most other advanced, industrialised states.

Conclusion

The British economy underwent severe trauma during the period between 1916 and 1940. It performed sluggishly for much of the period. Government (perhaps wisely) was reluctant to get too closely involved in matters like providing work or directing industrial restructuring. The results were often grim, but it must be remembered that the economy did go into the war with Germany just about strong enough to sustain the war effort - for a time, at least - and that Britain's economic ills in the period were not as great, or as potentially destabilising, as those of its major competitors, Germany and the United States. For all its problems - and they were many and real - the British economy did manage to deliver rising living standards to most of the British people during this period.

Questions to Consider
- What were the main effects of the operation of trade cycle in inter-war Britain?
- Why was unemployment so high between the wars?
- Could governments have done more to reduce unemployment?
- How important were the 'new' industries?
- What were the political effects of Britain's economic experience in this period?

9 Foreign Policy, 1918-40

Introduction

In 1914, Britain controlled a massive empire, dominated the world's finance and commerce, and remained one of the three leading industrial powers. This position of strength was apparently confirmed, albeit at great cost, by victory in the First World War. However, the diplomatic canvas upon which Britain had to work after 1918 was very different from the one to which it had previously been accustomed. It would need to make a peace which protected British interests, and then conduct its diplomacy so as to defend those interests. The fact that, just 21 years later, Britain was back at war with Germany suggested that inter-war diplomacy was not a great success, but it must be admitted that the problems with which British foreign policymakers were wrestling were massive and, in many cases, almost insoluble.

The Peace Conference

Having won the war, Britain's primary aims after 1918 was to ensure that such a conflict would not arise again, and to ensure that the balance of power was tipped permanently in its own favour. At the Paris peace conference of 1919, however, Britain was unable to have things all its own way, although it did, eventually, achieve a peace settlement which was, broadly, to its liking.

Lloyd George's freedom of action in Paris was constrained in a number of ways. Although the defeated Central Powers were not allowed representation, any peace settlement had to be enforceable. This meant that extreme solutions, such as the partition of Germany, were ruled out: fear of revolution was rife, and war-weariness meant that prolonged military occupation of Germany, which would be necessary to enforce partition, was impracticable. Although the peace settlement has usually been seen as harsh on the Central Powers, it could not be so harsh as to provoke Germany into renewed resistance, or into successful revolution.

Second, the British had not fought and won the war unaided, and their allies' views had, therefore, to be taken into account. While the Italians were ignored to the extent that they soon began to see themselves as victims, rather than victors, the views of the French and, especially, the Americans could not be dealt with in such a cavalier fashion. The French, perhaps understandably, were keen on revenge and on trying to ensure that they would never again face an attack from Germany. This inclined them towards a harsh peace settlement which would permanently weaken their eastern neighbour. On the other hand, the American President, Wilson, was keen on a 'just' peace settlement: his Fourteen Points had spoken of a liberal peace without annexations or indemnities.

Finally, the British government was constrained by what the British public was likely to accept. The 1918 general election had been fought by most government candidates on a fairly stern anti-German, patriotic ticket: many members of the cabinet were strongly in favour of a tough peace settlement and a significant extension of British power and influence to boot. Yet, paradoxically, these were both things which would involve, at least in the short term, a large input of British money and military personnel; and, since both of these would keep taxes high, divert spending from domestic projects, and involve the maintenance of large armed forces and possibly conscription, they were unlikely to be broadly acceptable in anything but the short term.

The peace conference began on 18 January 1919. The terms worked out were presented to the Germans, on a non-negotiable basis, on 7 May, and the Treaty of Versailles was signed on 28 June. Further treaties were signed with the other defeated powers: Saint-Germain with Austria (10 September); Neuilly with Bulgaria (27 November); Trianon with Hungary (4 June 1920, following the defeat of the Hungarian Bolshevik Republic of Bela Kun); and Sèvres with Turkey (10 August 1920, although this proved unenforceable: see overleaf).

The Peace Treaties

- A League of Nations was established, to act as an international

Armistice talks at the Versailles Conference, 1918

● The Peace Treaties

organisation to achieve the peaceable solution of future conflicts; defeated powers were not, at first, admitted as members.

- Germany was ordered to cede territory to France, Belgium and Poland.
- Memel and Danzig were to be free cities under the League of Nations.
- Referenda were to be held to determine whether northern and central Schleswig and areas of East Prussia remained part of Germany.
- The Saar area was to be administered by the League of Nations for 15 years, with France using the coal mines during that period.
- The Allies were to occupy the Rhineland area for 15 years, after which it would be permanently demilitarised.
- All German colonies were confiscated, and handed over to one or other of the victorious powers to be administered as 'mandates' under the League.
- Germany's military potential was restricted by various provisions: it was to have an army of not more than 100,000 men; conscription was outlawed; the size of the navy was restricted drastically; military aircraft and tanks were prohibited.
- Under Article 231 (the 'War Guilt' clause) Germany accepted sole responsibility for the war.
- As a result of Article 231, the Germans were required to pay reparations to the Allies for the cost of the war.
- The treaties with Austria, Hungary and Bulgaria restricted the sizes of their respective armed forces, made them liable for reparations, and took territory from them. Austria was prohibited from unifying with Germany.

Turkey: The Problem Case

Under the Treaty of Sèvres, Turkey lost its Middle East possessions to Britain and France: Britain gained Palestine and Iraq. However, it also lost territory on mainland Turkey to Greece. The result was a nationalist upsurge in Turkey and nationalists under Mustafa Kemal fought against the Greeks. At first, Lloyd George encouraged the Greeks to press their claims. But the result was that British troops almost became embroiled in conflict with the Turks at Chanak in September 1922. This was a significant factor in steeling many Conservative MPs to withdraw their support for Lloyd George at the Carlton Club meeting in October 1922.

The fall of Lloyd George, and of the Sultan shortly afterwards, showed that Sèvres was a dead letter, and a new peace settlement was agreed at Lausanne in 1923. This repudiated many of Greece's claims but, significantly, British gains from Turkey were confirmed. Turkey, under Kemal, went to work on a major programme of internal modernisation; in international terms, it became reasonably unproblematic.

Document 9a. Locarno Treaty, 16 October 1925
The Heads of State of Germany, Belgium, France, Britain and Italy. ... Anxious to satisfy the desire for security and protection which animates the peoples upon whom fell the scourge of war of 1914-18 ... have ... agreed as follows: *Article 1* The High Contracting Parties collectively and severally guarantee ... the maintenance of the territorial *status quo* resulting from the frontiers between Germany and Belgium and between Germany and France and the inviolability of the said frontiers as fixed by or in pursuance of the treaty of Peace signed at Versailles on the 28th June 1919.

The 1920s

There were no such obvious difficulties in enforcing the other peace treaties; and the League of Nations came into being in January 1920, allbeit without the participation of the Americans, who had moved back into isolation and refused to ratify Versailles. Britain signalled its unwillingness, given America's withdrawal, to get too closely involved in continental affairs by refusing a treaty with France and offering no support to the French when, in 1923, they occupied the Rhineland in response to Germany's default on reparations' payments. The Conservative government spent most of 1923 trying to find a middle way between the two countries, although this proved difficult. Finally, the first Labour government played a major part in reaching international agreement to the Dawes Plan of 1924, which rescheduled German reparations' payments.

The era of good feelings which began with Dawes was further emphasised, in 1925, by the conclusion of the Locarno Pact. The main feature of the various treaties agreed at the Swiss resort was the agreement between Britain, France, Germany, Italy and Belgium to guarantee existing Franco-German and Belgo-German borders. It was noticeable that the British had refused to guarantee Germany's eastern borders, thus raising the prospect of revision at some point in the future. But Locarno seemed, at the time, to be a major step forward, since it marked Germany's willing acceptance of a significant part of the dictated Versailles settlement. It also paved the way for Germany's admittance to the League, which duly followed in 1926. It seemed that a new era of co-operation had been born, and hopes were raised that outstanding international problems would soon be resolved, a significant factor in encouraging British governments towards international approaches to economic difficulties (see Chapter 8).

By the mid-1920s, in fact, the British were in the unusual position of having no clear foreign threat to face. Relations with Germany and France were reasonably good, and those with Germany improved further with the conclusion of the Young Plan in 1929, which again scaled down reparations. Relations with Fascist Italy, also, were fair. There was some tension with the United States, but it was not seriously expected that this might lead to genuine conflict in anything but the very long term.

This lack of a clear foreign threat had important consequences. First, it meant that there was something of a relaxation of control over parts of the Empire. The attempt to create a closely controlled area from the Mediterranean to India was abandoned even before the demise of the Lloyd George Coalition, with the ending of the protectorate over Egypt in 1922. Attempts to create an Indian-style administration in Iraq were abandoned, and it became effectively independent. The government of India was liberalised somewhat, following the Montagu-Chelmsford reforms of 1919, although not to an extent which would satisfy the extreme nationalists in the Congress party, led by Mahatma Gandhi. And relations with the Dominions - Australia, New Zealand, Canada and South Africa - were loosened with the agreements made at the 1926 imperial conference (and later ratified by the 1931 Statute of Westminster), which stated that all the Dominions, and Britain, were equal and free under the Crown.

The second result of this lack of a clear foreign threat was the restatement by the Conservative government, in 1926, of the rule first declared in 1919, that the forces should operate on the assumption that there would be no major war for the next decade. This was restated in 1927, and adopted on a rolling basis in 1928. This, in turn, resulted in a significant reduction in defence expenditure and personnel.

Relations with the Soviet Union were more fraught, admittedly. The British government was hostile towards the Bolshevik revolution of November 1917, partly on ideological grounds, partly because the Bolsheviks confiscated British property in Russia, and mainly because the new government soon withdrew from the war against Germany. Intervention, either in the form of armed forces sent to Russia, or the arming of the Soviet regime's opponents, continued into 1920, but in 1921 a trade agreement was concluded. In 1924 the first Labour government established diplomatic relations with the Soviet state. However, the existence in Moscow of the headquarters of the Communist International - a sort of general staff of world revolution, of which the small British Communist party was a part - and continued Communist propaganda within the Empire meant that many Conservatives remained very hostile. Following a raid on the headquarters of the Anglo-Russian Co-operative Society in London in 1927 (the 'Arcos raid'), diplomatic relations were broken off. However, these were restored by the second Labour government in 1929.

The second Labour government prided itself on its foreign policy (see Chapter 5). It restored relations with Russia and agreed the Young Plan. Relations with the United States improved after a somewhat frosty period under the second Baldwin government. Henderson, as Foreign Secretary, was instrumental in getting agreement to an early Allied evacuation of the Rhineland. The London Naval Treaty of 1930 saw agreement on naval disarmament between Britain, Japan and the United States, although France and Italy were unable to accept the terms proposed. And, in May 1931, the

League of Nations finally agreed to convene the World Disarmament Conference that had been proposed at the Versailles Paris Peace Conference but about which little had been done since. It was appropriate that Henderson was elected as President of the new body, which was scheduled to meet for the first time in February 1932.

New Problems

The World Disarmament Conference seemed to many to offer great hope for the future. But its prospects were never very good, especially given the circumstances in which it met. By February 1932 the world had been in the grip of economic recession for more than two years, and this had led most countries to abandon economic internationalism for higher and higher tariffs. This economic nationalism had led to a general deterioration in international relations. In addition, the new National government was much less favourable towards the conference than its Labour predecessor had been. There was a general feeling of unease within the government towards the conference and, indeed, the League; this was hardly lessened by the fact that the Labour party leader at the election had been none other than Henderson, who was now president of the conference (and who remained, although not an MP, Labour party leader until October 1932). Although it would be unfair to blame it for the conference's failure, the British government did little to assure its success: indeed, it abandoned the ten year rule in 1932.

Soon the disarmament conference was something of a sideshow, and it was indefinitely adjourned in June 1934. This marked the stubbing out of the fag-end of the 1920s' era of hope in international relations. By now, indeed, Britain's former position of facing no serious threats was beginning to be eroded very seriously indeed, to the extent that, by the end of 1935, it faced not one, but three powers which seemed to offer potential for danger.

The first to emerge was Japan. During the First World War the British and Japanese had been allies, but in 1922 the Americans had made the ending of this alliance the condition of a naval agreement. From then onwards, Anglo-Japanese relations had deteriorated. This mattered, of course, because Britain had extensive interests in India and the Far East, and needed Japan to be at least neutral if these interests were to be secure. However, the signal of a new era came in September 1931, when Japanese forces invaded the Chinese province of Manchuria and proceeded to establish a puppet state, Manchuokuo. Britain sponsored the League's attempts to reach some kind of settlement, but these failed and Britain was left with the fear that Japan was now a serious threat to its interests in the Far East. Such fears were merely reinforced, in December 1934, when Japan denounced the 1922 and 1930 naval agreements.

Second, the situation within Germany changed dramatically, with the coming to power of Adolf Hitler and the Nazi party, in January 1933.

Hitler, although a rabid anti-Communist and enemy of the Soviet Union, had in fact spent much of his rise to power attacking the Western powers and Versailles. His stiff attitude was emphasised when, in October 1933, Germany announced that it was withdrawing from the League and from the disarmament conference. Then, in March 1935, the German government went further, denouncing the disarmament clauses of Versailles and reintroducing conscription. By this time it was already clear that the Germans were assembling an air force in direct contravention of Versailles. While there remained debate within Britain as to what all this meant, it was clear to all that the conciliatory attitudes of the 1920s were well and truly gone, and that Germany must be treated as being at least potentially a military threat. Significantly, British rearmament began in 1935.

The third power to have emerged as a potential enemy by late 1935 was Italy. In some ways this was surprising. Anglo-Italian relations had been reasonable for most of the period since Mussolini had come to power in 1922. His Fascism posed no real obstacle to decent relations: the view taken was that Mussolini was a force for order and that foreign policy should be about defending British interests, not foisting its political system on other nations, particularly if the threat of Communism lurked in the background. Such good relations merely seemed to be sealed when, in April 1935 and in response to the German denunciation of Versailles, British, French and Italian representatives met at Stresa. They agreed to establish a common approach (the 'Stresa Front') towards Germany. Such an approach had much potential, or so it seemed: it was unlikely that Hitler would make serious military moves if confronted by a common front of three powers.

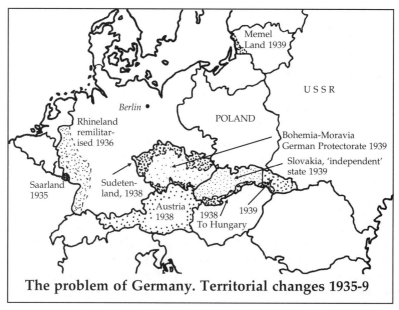

The problem of Germany. Territorial changes 1935-9

The Stresa Front then collapsed, however. The first body blow it suffered was the Anglo-German Naval Agreement of June 1935 (it restricted Germany's navy to 35 per cent the size of Britain's). While understandable in one sense, this clearly breached Stresa. Worse was to follow. During the summer, it became clear that the Italians were planning an invasion of the independent African state of Abyssinia (Ethiopia). Abyssinia was a member of the faltering League of Nations. In Britain, much of public opinion was appalled at this attack on a largely defenceless country. What few people noted was that this was how Britain had attained most of its Empire, but that point can be left to one side in the present discussion. It was an election year, and pro-League sympathy in Britain seemed to be strong. Hence, in September 1935, the Foreign Secretary, Hoare, made a strong speech to the League Assembly pledging Britain to support the League in defence of Abyssinian independence. Unperturbed, the Italians launched their invasion on 3 October. Eight days later the League voted to impose sanctions on Italy.

Sanctions soon proved ineffectual, and later attempts to beef them up by including oil were to falter - most countries gradually realised that such a step might mean war. In Britain, the National government won the election of November 1935 and soon set about looking for a settlement. The Hoare-Laval Pact was the result. But public outcry led to its abandonment (see Chapter 6).

The Abyssinian affair was soon overshadowed by other events, most notably the German remilitarisation of the Rhineland in March 1936. The Italians finally conquered Abyssinia that May; sanctions were terminated two months later. The Italians, who little more than a year earlier had been prepared to stand with Britain and France against Germany at Stresa, and who, the year before that, had mobilised their army to deter Germany from attempting to annex Austria, were now alienated. In August 1936 they formed an alliance with Germany (the Rome-Berlin Axis). Italy had been added to Japan and Germany as a potential threat to British interests.

The Approach of War

In retrospect, Mussolini's conquest of Abyssinia was to look like merely the start of a general Fascist advance during the latter half of the 1930s. The trend appeared to continue with the outbreak of the Spanish Civil War in July 1936, when a group of right-wing army officers began a rebellion against the democratic republican government, a struggle which culmina-ted, ultimately, in victory for General Franco and the 'Nationalists' in March 1939. Britain's role in the Spanish conflict was essentially negative: the government attempted to ensure that other powers followed its lead and did not intervene. However, the Germans, Italians and Soviets all intervened on a large scale.

But for all the tragedy involved in Spain, the most significant threat to

Britain in the later 1930s came from Germany. A sequence of events took place which carried Germany towards war, although the sequence is easier to see as such in retrospect than perhaps it was at the time. The remilitarisation of the Rhineland, in March 1936, was something of a short-lived crisis: once it had been done, few people thought it worth making much of a fuss. However, it did signal, once more, Hitler's potential for upsetting the diplomatic applecart, and British rearmament was intensified, although not as much as some people, like Churchill, would have liked. Government expenditure on defence rose from £113 million in 1934 to £136 million in 1935, £186 million in 1936, £265 million in 1937 and £400 million in 1938.

The next major crisis came in March 1938, when Germany annexed Austria in the *Anschluss*. Again, however, protest was muted. There was some feeling that Austria was not viable as an independent state, and much evidence of Austrian willingness to join with its larger neighbour.

A more serious crisis came in September 1938, when it became clear that Hitler intended to bring into the Reich the predominantly German-speaking area of Czechoslovakia, known as the Sudetenland (see map, page 92). At one point it seemed that, despite the efforts of the British Prime Minister, Chamberlain, Britain and Germany would go to war over the issue. However, Chamberlain was reluctant to start a conflict over, as he put it in a radio broadcast, 'a quarrel in a far-away country between people of whom we know nothing' (see Chapter 6). Despite the failure of two previous meetings with Hitler he was able to persuade Mussolini to convene the Munich conference, at which Britain, Germany, France and Italy agreed to compel Czechoslovakia to cede the Sudetenland to Germany.

Hitler victoriously enters the Sudetenland, 1938

Documents 9b. Agreement signed by Chamberlain and Hitler on 30 September 1938, after the Munich conference
We, the German Führer and Chancellor, and the British Prime Minister, have had a further meeting to-day, and are agreed in recognising that the question of Anglo-German relations is of the first importance for the two countries and for Europe. We regard the agreement signed last night, and the Anglo-German Naval agreement, as symbolic of the desire of our two peoples never to go to war with one another again.

9c. Chamberlain, to the crowds in Downing Street after his return from Munich, 30 September 1938
This is the second time in our history that there has come back from Germany to Downing Street peace with honour. I believe it is peace for our time.

9d. Churchill, debate on Munich agreement, House of Commons, October 1938
We have sustained a total and unmitigated defeat. ... And do not suppose that this is the end. It is only the beginning of the reckoning. This is only the first sip, the first foretaste of a bitter cup which will be proffered to us year by year unless, by a supreme recovery of moral health and martial vigour, we arise again and take our stand for freedom as in the olden time.

If Chamberlain hoped that this would prove to be the end of Hitler's territorial ambitions, he was soon proved wrong, for in March 1939 the Germans marched into Prague and annexed the Czech areas of what had been Czechoslovakia, and set up Slovakia as a separate puppet state. This was soon followed by the German annexation of Memel.

Faced with the prospect of rebellion within his own cabinet, and disquiet among a minority of Conservative MPs, Chamberlain now agreed to negotiations in Moscow with the Soviet Union for a pact against Germany. However, the British approach to the talks was lethargic, the delegation contained no leading political figures, and little progress was made. A lot more progress was made by the Germans; and on 23 August Germany and the Soviet Union signed a non-aggression pact, to widespread disbelief (they were, after all, supposedly sworn enemies from opposite sides of the political spectrum). On 1 September, Germany, freed from the fear of Soviet intervention, invaded Poland, whose borders had been guaranteed by Britain the previous March. Two days later Britain and France declared war on Germany. The Second World War had begun.

Why Appeasement?

During the period of Neville Chamberlain's premiership (May 1937 onwards), British foreign policy was characterised by what was known as Appeasement. This was, and remains, a hugely controversial issue. The premises upon which Appeasement were based were as follows:

- Britain was faced with a number of challenges - from Japan and Italy as well as Germany - and could not afford the possibility of conflict with all of these at once, so it made sense to reduce tensions where possible.

- Hitler, while in many ways a repulsive figure standing for abhorrent policies, was in other respects a traditional German nationalist who would be satisfied once all Germans were absorbed into the Reich.

- The peace settlement at Versailles had been fatally flawed and could not be upheld in all respects, so it made sense to revise it where this did not involve massive disruption or a fundamental challenge to vital British interests.

- Britain had just emerged from a long and hard depression - the last thing it needed was high spending on defence, which would mean higher taxes and interest rates and so, it was believed, plunge the economy back into crisis.

- There was no viable alternative - the League of Nations was effectively finished, and the weakness of the French and the weakness and untrustworthiness of the Russians meant that there was no possibility of a real coalition of powers to resist Germany by force.

- Britain was unprepared for war in 1938, in terms of civil defence as well as war materials and personnel.

- A successful resolution of the troubles of the Continent, achieved without resource to armed conflict, would give the National government a significant boost in readiness for the general election expected in late 1939 or early 1940.

These arguments were powerful, and Chamberlain had little difficulty in carrying his colleagues with him on the basis of them until after the Sudetenland crisis in autumn 1938.

There were critics, however. The Labour party, which had flirted with pacifism earlier in the 1930s and which, up to 1937, had opposed the defence estimates in Parliament, had emerged by late 1938 as a stern opponent of Appeasement, arguing for collective security through the League which, in essence, meant an Anglo-Franco-Soviet alliance against the Germans. In addition, a minority of Conservative MPs emerged as strong critics of Chamberlain. These included Churchill, although he was seen by many as a rather eccentric figure. More 'respectable' critics also emerged, though, such as Amery and Eden. Perhaps more importantly still, after Munich the Foreign Secretary, Lord Halifax, began to shift against Appeasement. This meant, ultimately, that Chamberlain's own freedom of manoeuvre within the cabinet was gravely weakened.

Some of the key arguments of the anti-appeasers were as follows:

- Britain had a moral obligation to defend the rights of the Czechs, Poles and other states that they had helped to create in 1919.

- Hitler was not a traditional German statesman, but a fanatic bent on world domination, as *Mein Kampf* showed.

- Delay in challenging Hitler would only make Britain's relative

weakness in defence terms all the greater.
- An alliance with the Soviets, while unpalatable to many, was preferable to allowing Hitler free rein in central and eastern Europe.

Essentially, what happened in the 11 months between Munich and the German invasion of Poland was that the arguments of the appeasers became less and less convincing. Despite Chamberlain's continuing desire to appease Hitler, he lost ground in the country, in his party and even within his own cabinet. The result was that, when the German invasion of Poland came, there seemed to be no realistic alternative to a declaration of war.

Conclusion

Britain's fundamental diplomatic problem between the wars was that it lacked the resources to pursue its preferred policy in all areas. This had been recognised as a problem even before 1914. However, the dynamics of post-war diplomacy, abetted by the unusual prominence of rampant imperialists in the higher reaches of the government, had pushed Britain to extend its commitments even further. This might have made sense at the time, and it did bring Britain significant advantages, especially in the Middle East. However, it also meant that Britain had more to defend than ever before, at a time when its resources were stretched and when the economy was not, for the most part, performing very well. This did not matter so much in the 1920s, when relations with Germany were good, and the only real threat that could be discerned was that of a rather weak Soviet Union. However, as the balance of world politics shifted in the 1930s, Britain found its position increasingly exposed. The result was that it was forced to shift from disarmament to rearmament, and to face up to the challenge of Nazi Germany. By September 1939 it appeared that what had been the peace to end all wars had been merely a truce presaging a new and even bigger conflict.

Questions to Consider
- Did Britain get the best settlement possible in the peace conference in 1919?
- What were the successes and failures of British foreign policy in the 1920s?
- How far was British foreign policy in the early 1930s characterised by drift and indecision?
- What were the main reasons for Chamberlain's pursuit of Appeasement?
- What alternatives were there to a policy of Appeasement, and why was none of them followed?

10 Historians and the Inter-war Period

Traditional Interpretations

The Second World War ended in 1945. In the two decades that followed, there was surprisingly little dispute about the history of Britain between 1916 and 1940. The view that was passed down to the future was a grim one. Britain had been run by at best muddled, and at worst criminally incompetent, politicians. The Conservative party had achieved its political dominance largely through trickery and the Labour party had been kept out of office by this and by the failings of its own leaders, most notably MacDonald. The fall of Lloyd George in 1922 had been followed until 1940, in Charles Mowat's memorable phrase in his book *Britain Between the Wars* (1955), by 'the rule of the pygmies, of the "second-class brains"' who allowed the country to 'sink in the hopeless morass of depression and unemployment', the 'lesser men' who 'frittered away Britain's power in the world'. Foreign policy had been run at first incompetently and then, under Chamberlain, with an almost wilful disregard for British interests. The economy's performance had been poor, and governments had been foolish not to see that Keynesian economics could have produced full employment. In their social policies generally, inter-war governments had been mean, penny-pinching and indifferent to the mass suffering experienced for much of the inter-war period by the bulk of the population. It was a damning indictment. Why did it take hold with such force?

The first reason is that things were very much better in the two decades following the war. Unemployment, which had never fallen below a million between 1920 and 1940, and had, at one point, reached around three times that figure, did not exceed 500,000 between 1945 and 1958 or 700,000 before 1971 (with a very brief exception in 1947). Governments were practising Keynesian economics, or so it was thought. The conclusion was irresistible. If Keynesian economics created full employment in post-war Britain, then they could have done so in the period between the wars. Those who had refused to listen to Keynes, or not voted for Lloyd George in 1929, or failed to support Mosley in 1930, were either fools or knaves. It was really as simple as that.

Second, those who might have been expected to mount some kind of defence of the performance of inter-war governments were, for various reasons, unable or unwilling to do so. Chamberlain died in 1940, Baldwin in 1947. Their closest colleagues were mostly apologetic in their memoirs, fearing that they would be blamed for Britain's perceived weakness by 1939.

Third, critics of inter-war governments were in a strong position to be heard. One might have expected the leadership of the Conservative party to have defended the party's record between the wars. Yet the party took its smashing electoral defeat in 1945 as a lesson that it should draw a line under the inter-war period and move on to the future. And the party's leaders until 1963, Churchill, Eden and Macmillan, had all been rebels during the 1930s, and so were hardly likely to defend vigorously - if at all - the records of Baldwin and Chamberlain. Indeed, Churchill's own six-volume history of the war, particularly the first volume which dealt with the 1930s - *The Gathering Storm* (1948) - was a slashing critique which was to dominate historians' thinking on foreign policy, in particular, for a generation.

Fourth, few professional historians were writing about inter-war Britain before the 1960s. Those who did largely had the field to themselves, and could make what seem now to be rash judgements without too much fear of contradiction. In most cases, their political views were such that they favoured either a pro-Labour or a Churchillian view of the inter-war period; neither of these was likely to give those years a rosy tinge.

Finally, and one cause of this professional neglect, the official papers remained largely secret and unavailable for research. Government papers were classified for 50 years after their production, and without the close attention to policymaking which they would have allowed, it is unsurprising that sweeping - condemnatory - judgements continued to hold the field.

Revisionist Views

In 1967, Robert Skidelsky published his *Politicians and the Slump*, a scholarly work which condemned the second Labour government for not adopting a Keynesian approach towards the economy and unemployment in particular. However, the tide among historians was already beginning to turn in the opposite direction. The period between then and the late 1970s was to be dominated, so far as inter-war Britain was concerned, with a flood of works which revised favourably the performance of government and the economy, and which questioned the old stereotyped view that the period between the wars had been ones of unremitting grimness.

There were revisionist biographies. Keith Middlemas and John Barnes published their massive, and sympathetic, life of Baldwin in 1969; David Marquand's book on MacDonald followed in 1977. Within five years of Churchill's death, Robert Rhodes James boldly wrote a strong critique of the wartime hero's pre-war record in *Churchill: A Study in Failure, 1900-1939* (1970). Revisionist accounts of economic performance also appeared, with H.W. Richardson (in *Economic Recovery in Britain, 1932-1939* (1967)) going so far as to argue that the inter-war economy had been essentially vibrant and the new industries emerging as a 'development block' especially in the 1930s. In a most important article published in 1975 (and reprinted in his 1990 book, *Ideologies of Class*), Ross McKibbin took apart the Skidelsky thesis on the second Labour government's economic policy, a trend which has been followed since, in a number of articles and books, by the economic historian Alan Booth, among others. Views of a Britain of almost unremitting grimness during the inter-war period were challenged forcefully by the work of John Stevenson and Chris Cook in their book *The Slump* (1977). And even Appeasement began to find defenders. In an important article published in 1976, for example, Paul Schroeder argued that the policy was in keeping with traditional British policies, and so was not some error forced upon an unwilling country by a crazed Chamberlain but a rational policy whose worth appeared, to the premier, to have been proven by the test of time. Three years later George Peden's book *British Rearmament and the Treasury, 1932-1939*, showed how serious had been the economic and financial constraints on British rearmament during the Thirties.

It would be foolish to argue that no one stuck to the older traditional line during this period, of course. Nevertheless, the revisionists were now producing much the most important work, and there had clearly been a sea-change in historians' attitudes, taken as a whole, towards the inter-war period.

There were three basic reasons for this change. First, the contemporary context was very different from that which had prevailed until the early or mid 1960s. Government is never easy, but it seemed to become much more difficult from the later 1960s onwards. This, in turn, suggested that inter-war ministers had not been incompetent, just faced with numerous, almost insoluble, problems; and their record began to be compared favourably with that of their successors in the Labour and Conservative governments of the 1960s and 1970s. Keynesian economics, too, began to appear increasingly problematic as inflation and unemployment began to rise together despite government's attempts to remain within a Keynesian framework. It began to be seen, in fact, that British prosperity between the late 1940s and the early 1960s had been due, primarily, to temporary or world factors and not so much to policy initiatives on the part of British governments. In short, Keynesian economics began to be seen as problematic in the contemporary world, and so there was a good deal of sympathy with those who had been sceptical about them between the wars. Finally, the making of external policy became harder and harder as Britain tried to adjust to a diminishing world role and the challenge of European integration: again, this led historians to be more sympathetic to the earlier period, and to see better the very real problems that inter-war foreign policymakers had had to face.

The second reason for the change was the greater availability of original documents. In 1967, the 30 year rule was adopted regarding the secrecy of government documents, in place of the 50 year rule. This meant that, within a very short time, the bulk of government documents for the inter-war period were declassified. At the same time, the private papers of politicians and other policymakers began to be opened up. As historians worked on the original documents, they realised, to a much greater extent than before, the complexities of policymaking in inter-war Britain; they also became, in many cases, far more intimate with, and sympathetic towards, the historical characters they were studying. Finally, the dying off of old protagonists allowed historians greater leeway. It was inconceivable, for example, the Rhodes James's book could have been published while Churchill was still alive.

Post-Revisionism

From the late 1970s, however, the trend became less clear. Some historians continued to argue that inter-war governments had been effective, by and large; that the economy had been reasonably buoyant; that living standards had risen; and that foreign policy had been rational and sensible, even if not always terribly effective. Trenchant defenders of the record of inter-war governments could still be found, as with John Charmly's *Chamberlain and the Lost Peace* (1991), which presented a vigorous defence of Appeasement, or the present author's *Britain in the 1930s* (1992), which offered a basically 'optimistic' view of that decade. Other historians, however, having absorbed the revisionists' views, now began to counter-attack. The arguments of Stevenson and Cook about rising living standards, for example, were strongly questioned in a series of articles by the medical historian, Charles Webster. W.R. Garside reiterated and deepened the Keynesian critique of unemployment policy in his *British Unemployment, 1919-1939* (1990). And R.A.C. Parker's *Chamberlain and Appeasement* (1993), while seeing the rationale for Appeasement and engaging fully with the arguments of those who had defended it, still concluded that the government, and particularly Chamberlain himself, did have choices but that it made the wrong ones, and so 'probably stifled serious chances of preventing the Second World War'. The debates, in short, go on, and will continue to do so.

Students and Changing Views

If all historians agreed about everything then there would not need to be further history books on the same topic, and there would not need to be so many historians. Even so, they do not argue with each other just for the sake of it. As the Labour politician, Aneurin Bevan, once said, 'there are no arguments in a graveyard', and the fact that historians do differ so strongly, and sometimes passionately, about British history between 1916 and 1940 shows that it is a lively and exciting subject to study.

But does it matter to students? Why should a student take the trouble to go further than this book and try to find out what it is that makes historians differ? It is because of the nature of the subject. History is not a collection of facts. It is a matter of interpretation, of selection of evidence, and the development of an argument. If another historian had written this book, for example, it would be different. At a banal level, the chapters would have different titles. More seriously, the emphasis might have been less on political history, or more favourable towards Lloyd George, or taken a less optimistic view of social and economic progress, or whatever. As the rest of this chapter has shown, historians differ because they write in different times. They also have different political views, or different sets of moral values.

The main point for the student is that they should try to see where historians are coming from, and view all their arguments with a critical eye. Try to work out why historians differ in their views of the past. Once you have worked out the preconceptions and biasses of your historians, you will be in a much stronger position to work out your own views of past events. And, above all else, remember that, to put it crudely, a professional historian is only someone who has read more books and documents than you. None of us was born knowing the dates of the Prime Ministers, or steel production figures, and so on, off by heart. The day that all students begin to believe uncritically everything that they read or are told by historians is the day that the discipline of History will die.

11 Britain in 1940: Continuity and Change

The superficial parallels between the start and end of the period covered by this book are striking. In 1940, as in 1916, Britain was at war with Germany, fighting a desperate war of survival. In 1940, as in 1916, it had a new Prime Minister who was much distrusted by some but whose energy and dynamism seemed to many others a welcome contrast from the apparent failings of their predecessors. In 1940, as in 1916, the war seemed to offer opportunities, as well as threats: opportunities for further social change, and a chance of real political change. And in 1940, as in 1916, Britain was hoping that the Americans would intervene on their side.

The period between 1916 and 1940 had been marked by many continuities. The parliamentary system remained intact. Capitalism still prevailed, and there had been only limited movement towards a more interventionist role for the State in economic affairs. Britain still saw itself as essentially a Christian country, even if a rather smaller percentage of the population now went to church regularly. Class divisions remained, and so too did splits within the main social classes.

Yet, at the same time, there had been significant changes. The great Liberal party, which had dominated politics for much of the period between the 1832 Reform Act and the outbreak of war in 1914, was a powerless, rudderless and tiny rump. The Conservatives, who had been in such difficulties before the First World War, had been in office, either alone or in Coalition, for all but three of the 24 years of the period. Labour, meanwhile, had grown from a somewhat marginal pressure group to emerge as the second party in the State, and had had its first tastes of government. In society, it would not be exaggerating to talk of a leisure and mass communications revolution. And living standards had risen for most people.

Of course, the war was eventually won, although largely due to American and Soviet efforts. In 1945, peace with Germany was followed by a sweeping electoral victory for the Labour party under Attlee, and in the six years that followed there were significant changes which seemed to many at the time, and have seemed to many historians since, to mark little less than a democratic revolution. By 1951, when Labour left office, there had been all kinds of changes: about 20 per cent of industry had been nationalised; full employment had been maintained; social security had been shaken up; the National Health Service had been created. The 'Welfare State' was now deemed by most to be a reality, and was not to be seriously challenged for almost three decades. The economy, buffeted by the years of war and reconstruction, was now set fair for a long period of growing prosperity that tended to put the unspectacular performance of the inter-war years in the shade. And the North Atlantic Treaty Organisation (NATO), formed in 1949, for the first time in peacetime committed the United States to the defence of western Europe.

And yet, in other ways, the post-war period was to see the continuation of many of the processes that had been taking place before the Second World War. Britain's share of international trade, and hence its economic importance and power, continued to shrink. Its role as a world power was further reduced as the dominance of the two 'superpowers', the United States and the USSR, became obvious. Even here, though, the pattern can be oversimplified. While the Labour government gave independence to India, it had no master plan for the end of the Empire: at various stages it had hoped to exploit the Empire more effectively in order to increase British living standards and military might. Even in the early 1950s Colonial Office officials were talking of it being several generations before some colonies would be even considered for independence. These extra-European commitments, and the sense of a 'special relationship' with the United States, were to prevent Britain from becoming too closely involved in moves towards a degree of western European integration, with the result that Britain was not a member of the European Economic Community when it was formed in 1957, and indeed did not join until 1973. The tensions inherent in Britain's position between its one-time world dominance and its fate as a rather marginal regional power were to pose as many problems, ultimately, for post-war politicians as they had been for their predecessors. But that, as they say, is another story.

Further Reading

1. Textbooks covering the whole or part of the period

C.L. Mowat, *Britain Between the Wars, 1918-1940* (1955) and A.J.P. Taylor, *English History 1914-45* (1965) are the classic textbooks but are showing their age and should not be relied upon. The essays in P. Catterall (ed.), *Britain 1918-1951* (1994) are aimed specifically at post-GCSE students. M. Pugh, *State and Society: British Political and Social History 1870-1992* (1994), P.F. Clarke, *Hope and Glory: Britain 1900-1992* (1996) and K. Robbins, *The Eclipse of a Great Power: Britain 1870-1992* (1994) all cover a longer period but have much of value to say about 1916-40. There is a good collection of essays in P. Johnson (ed.), *Twentieth Century Britain: Economic, Social and Cultural Change* (1994). The latter half of the period is covered in J. Stevenson and C. Cook, *Britain in the Depression: Society and Politics, 1929-1939* (1994) (first published as *The Slump* (1977)) and A. Thorpe, *Britain in the 1930s* (1992). Basic statistical and other information is contained in A. Thorpe, *The Longman Companion to Britain in the Era of the World Wars, 1914-1945* (1994); more detail, should it be needed, can be found in B.R. Mitchell, *British Historical Statistics* (1988) and A.H. Halsey (ed.), *British Social Trends since 1900* (1988).

2. Politics

As well as the above, most of which say a great deal about the politics of the period, see M. Pugh, *The Making of Modern British Politics, 1867-1939* (1993). On specific parties, see the relevant sections of A. Thorpe, *History of the British Labour Party* (1997), J. Ramsden, *The Age of Balfour and Baldwin, 1902-1940* (1978) (on the Conservatives), and C. Cook, *A Short History of the Liberal Party, 1900-1992* (1993). There are few really good, short and accessible biographies of the leading political figures of the period; exceptions are M. Pugh, *Lloyd George* (1988) and K. Robbins, *Churchill* (1992).

3. The Economy

S. Pollard, *The Development of the British Economy, 1914-1980* (1983) and D.H. Aldcroft, *The British Economy Between the Wars* (1983) are both good introductions. For more detail on policy, see A. Booth and M. Pack, *Employment, Capital and Economic Policy: Great Britain, 1918-1939* (1985) and W.R. Garside, *British Unemployment, 1919-1939* (1990).

4. Society

J. Stevenson, *British Society 1914-1945* is the best overall view. Accessible works on the various subjects covered in Chapter 7 are as follows: N. Tranter, *British Population in the Twentieth Century* (1996); H. Jones, *Health and Society in Twentieth-Century Britain* (1994); H. Perkin, *The Rise of Professional Society: England since 1880* (1989); D. Beddoe, *Back to Home and Duty: Women Between the Wars, 1918-1939* (1989); B. Simon, *The Politics of Educational Reform, 1920-1940* (1974); A. Hastings, *History of English Christianity, 1920-1990* (1991); and S.G. Jones, *Workers at Play: A Social and Economic History of Leisure 1918-1939* (1986).

5. Foreign Policy

Important and accessible works include P.M. Kennedy, *The Realities Behind Diplomacy: Background Influences on British External Policy 1865-1980* (1981) and D. Reynolds, *Britannia Overruled: British Policy and World Power in the Twentieth Century* (1991). Specifically on Appeasement, contrast the views of J. Charmly, *Chamberlain and the Lost Peace* (1991) with those of R.A.C. Parker, *Chamberlain and Appeasement: British Policy and the Coming of the Second World War* (1993). K. Robbins, *Appeasement* (1988) remains a useful survey.

Index

Abdication Crisis   12, 14, 53-4
Abyssinia   6, 7, 51, 93
Amery, Leopold   39, 48, 82, 96
Anglo-German naval treaty   7, 93, 95
Anschluss   94
Appeasement   12, 13, 55-7, 95-7, 100, 101
aristocracy   62
Asquith, Herbert Henry   4, 10, 11, 14, 17, 20, 30, 36, 81
Astor, Lady   4, 64
Attlee, Clement   7, 51, 52, 57, 103
Austria   4, 7, 19, 88, 94

Baldwin, Stanley   5-7, 12, 25, 27-9, 31, 32, 36, 37, 39, 42, 43, 48, 49, 51, 53, 54, 68, 98, 99
Balfour, Arthur   10
Beaverbrook, Lord   39, 53
benefits   41, 50, 83
Birkenhead, Lord   21, 25, 32
Black Friday   4, 23
Bondfield, Margaret   27, 64
Brest-Litovsk, Treaty of   19
British Union of Fascists   6, 39, 49, 50
budget   6, 38, 40, 43, 45, 66, 81, 82
Bulgaria   19, 88

Campbell Case   5, 31
Chamberlain, Austen   21, 22, 25, 32
Chamberlain, Neville   7, 13, 28, 32, 33, 39, 41, 43, 44, 48, 50, 51, 53-7, 94-8, 100
Chanak Incident   5, 25, 88
Chelmsford, Lord   29, 90
Churchill, Winston   7, 13, 21, 25, 32, 33, 36, 43, 48
cinema   68, 70, 72
class   8, 9, 59, 60, 61-3, 72, 100, 103
coal   2, 4, 5, 8, 21, 23, 34, 35, 62, 75, 77-8
Coalition government, 1916-18   1, 4, 17-19
Coalition government, 1918-22   4, 20-6, 90
Communist party   2, 4, 31, 49, 84, 90
conscription   4, 17, 87, 88, 92
Conservative government, 1922-3   5, 27-8, 89
Conservative government, 1924-9   5, 32-7, 75, 90
Conservative party   4, 5, 10, 13, 14, 17, 20, 21, 24, 26-31, 37, 39, 40, 44-52, 56, 64, 75, 81, 81, 82, 96, 98, 103
Curzon, Lord   12, 27, 28, 32

Dawes Plan   5, 82, 89
depressed/special areas   6, 50, 51, 57, 79, 83, 84
economic policy   30, 39, 42, 43, 50, 51, 59, 79, 81-5, 98, 100
economic structure   9, 76-81
economy   1-3, 21, 31, 34, 36, 38, 51, 55, 57, 66, 73, 74, 91, 96, 97, 99, 101, 104
Eden, Anthony   7, 52, 55, 96, 99
education   21, 24, 39, 62, 64, 65-6, 72
Edward VIII   7, 14, 52
Empire   3, 11, 25, 86, 90, 93, 104
engineering   2, 8, 34, 63
First World War   2, 17, 58, 64, 65, 71, 76, 78, 91, 103
Fisher, H.A.L.   65
France   1, 2, 4, 7, 11, 17, 19, 28, 86, 88, 89, 93, 95, 96
free trade   13, 14, 28, 29, 39, 42, 46, 48, 73, 81, 82

Gallacher, William   49
'Geddes Axe'   2, 24, 65
gender   37, 61, 63-5, 71
general elections   20, 27-9, 32, 36, 37, 45, 47, 51, 52, 75, 83, 87, 96, 99
General Strike   2, 5, 12, 34-5, 63, 75, 77
George V   7, 10, 41, 51, 52
German-Soviet Pact   7, 95
Germany   2, 4, 6-8, 11, 14, 17-19, 55, 56, 76, 83, 85, 86, 89, 91, 93-6, 103
gold standard   1, 5, 6, 22, 34, 40, 42-5, 47, 49, 75, 81-3
Greenwood, Arthur   38, 57

Halifax, Lord   7, 55-7, 96
health   60-1, 62, 64, 72, 104
Henderson, Arthur   4-6, 20, 29, 37, 38, 40, 44, 47, 65, 68, 90
Hoare, Sir Samuel   6, 51, 53, 93
Hoare-Laval Pact   7, 52, 93
hobbies   68, 71
holidays   55, 71
House of Lords   9-11, 28, 29, 66
housing   14, 21, 24, 36, 38, 62, 68, 83, 84

Independent Labour party   15, 47
India   6, 13, 14, 49, 51, 90, 91, 104
infant mortality   59-61
Ireland   1, 4, 5, 10, 11, 24, 32, 67
iron and steel   8, 78
Italy   2, 7, 51, 55, 58, 86, 89, 92, 93, 95
Japan   2, 38, 90, 91, 95
Jowett, Frederick   29

Joynson-Hicks, Sir William 36

Keynes, John Maynard 82-4, 98

Labour government, 1924 5, 29-32, 89

Labour government, 1929-31 6, 37-42, 55, 75, 82, 90, 99, 100

Labour party 1, 4, 5, 7, 10, 16, 17, 20, 23, 26-9, 31, 36, 37, 40, 41, 44-7, 51, 52, 56, 81, 82, 84, 91, 96, 98, 104

Lansbury, George 6, 47, 51

Lausanne, Treaty of 88

Law, Andrew Bonar 5, 10, 12, 21, 25, 27, 28, 33

League of Nations 6, 51, 87-9, 91-3, 96

leisure 68-71, 72, 104

Liberal National party 6, 44, 47, 48, 51, 52

Liberal party 1, 4-6, 10, 15, 17, 20, 26-9, 31, 36, 37, 39, 40-2, 44, 47, 48, 51, 52, 82, 84, 103

Lloyd George, David 3-5, 10, 13, 14-15, 17, 18, 21, 25-8, 31, 36, 37, 41, 43, 49-51, 53, 81, 84, 88, 98

Lloyd George Fund 15, 25, 36

Locarno Pact 5, 33, 36, 89

London Naval Treaty 6, 90

MacDonald, Ramsay 5, 6, 15-16, 20, 27, 29-31, 36-43, 45, 47-8, 51, 55, 98, 99

Maclean, Sir Donald 21

maternal mortality 60, 61, 64

Mosley, Sir Oswald 6, 38, 39, 49, 50, 84, 98

Munich Conference 7, 56, 94-7

national debt 28, 42, 73, 84

National government, 1931-5 2, 6, 41, 42, 47-51, 66, 75, 82, 83, 91

National government, 1935-7 2, 7, 51-4, 93

National government, 1937-40 54-7

nationalisation 23, 29, 30, 52, 77, 82, 103

National Labour party 41, 44, 47, 52

'new' industries 38, 73, 78, 79, 85, 100

nutrition 61

'Phoney War' 56, 57

Poland 2, 7, 56, 66, 88, 95, 97

population 8, 58-60

prices 18, 34, 74, 77

protection 13, 28-30, 33, 36, 37, 39, 45, 47, 48, 82

public works 15, 28, 50, 83

pubs 63, 68-9

radio 70, 72

railways 4, 21, 23

reading 63, 66, 68, 70-1

Reading, Lord 43

rearmament 55, 76, 85, 92, 94, 97, 100

Red Friday 5, 34

religion 5, 10, 32, 33, 39, 50, 63, 66-8, 103

rents 18, 21

Rothermere, Lord 49, 50

Runciman, Walter 45

Russia, Soviet Union 1, 2, 4, 5-7, 11, 17-19, 31, 36, 58, 83, 90, 93, 95-7, 104

sale of honours 15, 24

Samuel, Sir Herbert 5, 34, 41, 43, 49, 52

Scotland 10, 11, 68, 79

Second World War 2, 49, 60, 63, 65, 66, 72, 79, 95, 98, 101

Sèvres, Treaty of 87

sexually transmitted diseases 64

shipbuilding 34, 78

Simon, Sir John 44, 51

Sinclair, Sir Archibald 52

Snowden, Philip 6, 20, 27, 29, 30, 37, 38, 40, 43, 44, 46, 48, 82

socialism 4, 10, 21, 26, 29, 30, 36, 38, 52, 82

Spanish Civil War 7, 93

sport 68, 69

staple industries 8, 55, 76-9

Stresa Front 6, 92-3

Sudetenland 7, 94, 96

strikes 2, 18, 21, 23

tariffs 6, 28, 31, 39, 42, 44, 46, 48, 81, 82, 91

textiles 2, 8, 64, 78

Thomas, J.H. 23, 37, 38, 40, 43, 44, 53

trade cycle 73-6, 85

trade unions 5, 21, 23, 29, 32, 36, 63, 67

Trades Union Congress 5, 34, 35, 40

Trevelyan, C.P. 29, 66

Triple Alliance 21, 23

Turkey 1, 4, 13, 19, 21, 25, 88

unemployment 1, 6, 15, 22, 23, 28, 30, 36-8, 43, 46-51, 57, 59, 73-80, 82-5, 98, 101

United States 2, 4-8, 17-19, 28, 37, 38, 55, 70, 74-6, 83-7, 89-91, 103, 104

universities 65, 66

urbanisation 8, 9, 59, 60

Versailles, Treaty of 87, 89, 92, 96

Wales 10, 11, 50, 60, 62, 63, 68, 79

Webb, Sidney 29

Wheatley, John 29, 30

working class 9, 10, 19, 21, 23, 31, 61-3, 68, 69, 71

women 3, 5, 9, 21, 23, 63-5, 69, 70, 72, 73

World Disarmament Conference 6, 38

Young Plan 6, 82, 89, 90